FANCY AF

COCKTAILS

**ARIANA MADIX
& TOM SANDOVAL** / *with Danny Pellegrino*
Photography by Kelly Puleio / HOUGHTON MIFFLIN HARCOURT
BOSTON · NEW YORK · 2019

FANCY AF
COCKTAILS

Copyright © 2019 by Ariana Madix and Tom Sandoval

Photography © 2019 by Kelly Puleio

Production design by Maxwell Smith

Cocktail design by Mo Hodges

Production by Tamara Costa

Photo assisting by Nicola Parisi

Prop assisting by Avery Ferguson and Kelly Fallon

Hair styling by Bradley Leake

Makeup styling by Jared Lipscomb

For information about permission to reproduce selections from this book, write to trade.permissions@hmhco.com or to Permissions, Houghton Mifflin Harcourt Publishing Company, 3 Park Avenue, 19th Floor, New York, New York 10016.

hmhbooks.com

Library of Congress Cataloging-in-Publication Data is available.

ISBN 978-0-358-17171-3 (hbk)

ISBN 978-0-358-17198-0 (ebk)

Book design by Laura Palese

Printed in the United States of America

DOC 10 9 8 7 6 5 4 3 2 1

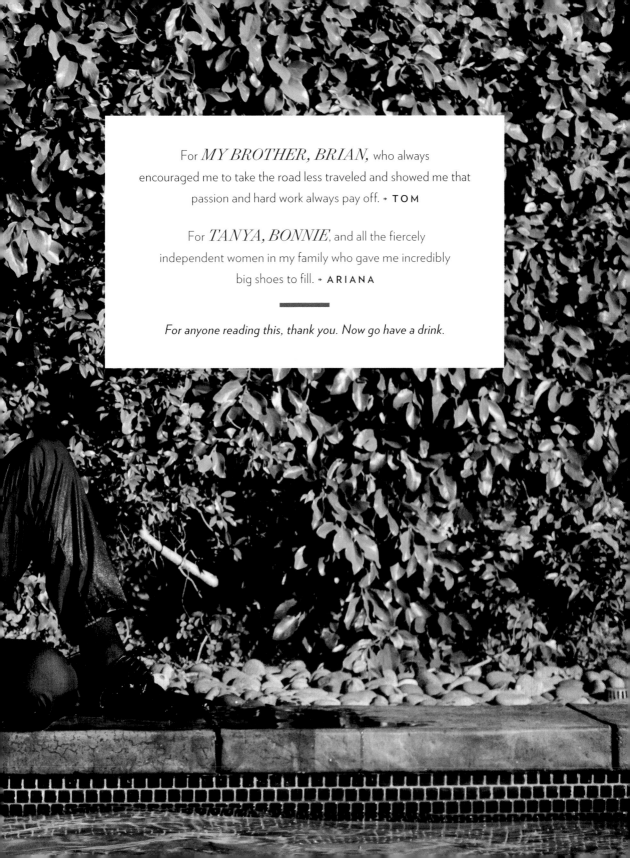

For *MY BROTHER, BRIAN,* who always encouraged me to take the road less traveled and showed me that passion and hard work always pay off. → **TOM**

For *TANYA, BONNIE,* and all the fiercely independent women in my family who gave me incredibly big shoes to fill. → **ARIANA**

———

For anyone reading this, thank you. Now go have a drink.

CONTENTS

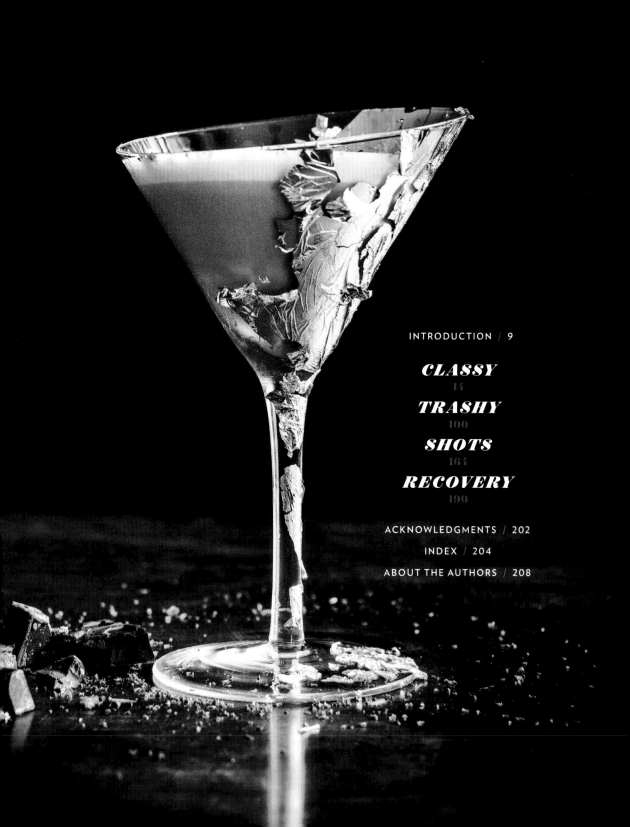

INTRODUCTION

We've talked about it, we've hinted at it, and after some delay and years in the making, our cocktail book is finally here! Most of you recognize us from *Vanderpump Rules* on Bravo. Season after season, you see us in the opening credits trying to look sexy, keep it together, and not blink while corks fly and the cocktails overflow around us. That doesn't mean we always actually look sexy. Let's be real: you've seen us at our highs and lows. You've seen our makeups and breakups, drunk vacations, and a few ugly cries. You've witnessed us trying to make music with trumpets and robot voices, crushing shit with bulldozers, and starting businesses. We've lost loved ones, fought over comedy, modeled in sexy restaurant photo shoots, and kicked doors in drag. And let's not forget our old friend, the lovely SUR dumpster. He's been right by our side through friendships starting, ending, starting again, heart to hearts, verbal castrations, cheating scandals, brownouts, blackouts, and a good ole puke-and-rally. Those opening credits are indicative of our show. Each episode starts with us looking classy and put together, but at some point we always look a trashy mess.

Even though we've ugly-cried, drank too much, overreacted, and underreacted, these often become our most unforgettable moments. We can be self-righteous, overly sardonic, and vain. We hear all those things you say about us on social media, and we don't always disagree. We're messy, but it's real. And so are the relationships. The show works, in our opinion, because we are all truly friends. We've lived together, worked together, and bled together way before cameras were ever rolling. There are a lot of other wonderfully compelling reality shows, but often it's clear that the friendships stop as soon as filming stops. We "never stop never stopping."

Before you saw any *Vanderpump Rules* relationships unfold, we were both bartenders. We worked in some of the most popular bars in New York, Chicago, Miami, and Los Angeles. We served drinks to celebrities, socialites, housewives, cool people, and definitely a few assholes. You learn a lot, slinging cocktails for the elite, the average Joe, and everyone in between. You learn what people like and what they don't like. You learn what flavors blend well and which don't. When it comes to life and our emotions we may be lacking, but when it comes to alcohol, and drinking . . . we are professionals. We know how to make great drinks because we've been making and drinking them for years. The delicious libations, creations, and mental masturbations you find in this book have been honed (and a little postponed), but are now ready. A few seasons back on the show, we started talking about a cocktail book. Everywhere we went, people would ask when it was coming. Truth is, throughout that time we were always creating new cocktails. We wanted them to be epic.

What we hear most often, aside from "What happened with the cocktail book?" or "Let's do shots," or "Tom was pretty in drag," or "It seems like you hate everyone, Ariana," is that people are surprised by how delicious the cocktails are at SUR, Villa Blanca, PUMP, and TomTom. We want people who pick up this book to feel that same sense of surprise and excitement when they make one of our drinks at home.

Every occasion is covered in this book. We include recipes that are perfect for black tie affairs, and others that are great for boozing solo in your sweatpants while live-tweeting your Bravo shows (#FancyAF). It's a mix of classy and trashy. We've had some of these in our finest garb alongside celebrities and socialites, and others we've mixed and consumed out of water bottles in one of our old, shitty apartments without central air. We like to think we're all a mix of classy and trashy, so we hope you enjoy the cocktails we've created.

With these recipes, there are some behind-the-scenes, never-been-told stories about the show and our personal lives. Ever wonder what happened *after* the infamous phone recording? We can tell you what happened when the cameras left after the fights broke out. Curious where the sidecar came from? We have that covered, too. More important than all that, the drinks are phenomenal. We've gotten wasted testing each and every one of these (multiple times) to ensure they are the best possible cocktails. It was a tough job, but someone had to do it. Some of these recipes are more advanced than others, but hopefully all of them make you more comfortable mixing drinks in your own home. We even included a few hangover/hair-of-the-dog recipes alongside the mixed drinks and shots, so you aren't hurting too much from the booze. So, grab your bar kit and get ready to drink like a pro. And leave yourself a 20% tip for a job well done.

Before we get started, remember to drink responsibly, or at least hide it well. We aren't the morality police, but don't f*cking drink and drive. And don't drink and rage-text. Generally, just don't be an asshole. Be smart, be safe, and know your limits.

Finally, it's tradition to say a few words before drinking with friends, so we want to leave you with a little toast . . .

Raise your glass high, this one's for you.

/ **XO**
/ **ARIANA & TOM**

GETTING STARTED

We have a few recipes in this book that are designed to be made with things you have around your house (or apartment/condo/dorm). However, there are quite a few that require materials you may not have. We put together our list of bar basics that will help you get started. Once you start mixing, you'll want to start playing around and customizing. You may even create something delicious that we couldn't even dream of. In our opinion, everyone over 21 should have these items at the bar so they can make a few drinks.

Ice Trays. There are so many fancy silicone trays out there. You don't need to spend a ton of money on an ice tray, but if you want to class it up a bit, you can buy one of the sphere trays. Spheres melt slower than the traditional cubes. One pound of ice per person is the general rule when making drinks. Some recipes taste better with crushed ice, so we noted that in the recipe.

Cocktail Shaker. We like the Boston-style cocktail shaker best. This means the shaking metal tin and the mixing glass are separate. A high-quality tin (28 ounce) with a glass (or acrylic, 16 ounce) will look good on your bar even when the juices have spilled everywhere. You can also use a mixing tin (18 ounce) to fit into the shaking metal tin (28 ounce). Both of these options allow you to put a separate strainer right on top. Using a glass or acrylic glass for mixing and muddling is preferred because you can see the ingredients. We do a lot of muddling and shaking, so acrylic is also the most durable. If you're looking to save money, you can usually find a great, Boston-style cocktail shaker bar kit at a discount store. Typically, those don't come with the mixing glass, but they will work for beginners and often have the strainer built in. Generally, when we say to "shake" the ingredients in cocktail shaker, you should shake to a count of ten. More will dilute the drink, and less won't properly mix the ingredients.

Strainer. Nothing too flimsy. Hawthorne-style if you're going with the Boston-style shaker.

Bar Spoon. 30 cm is standard for stirring.

Muddler. We muddle a lot. When you're working with things like herbs or fruits, the muddler will allow you to open up the flavors in the ingredients, so your drink tastes good. Get a muddler with plastic teeth; never metal because it breaks glass.

Jigger. This two-sided measuring cup will make following the recipes much easier. The more drinks you make, the more comfortable you'll be eyeballing measurements. Standard size is 1½ ounces on one side, and 1 ounce on the other. We like to have three different-sized jiggers, each a different color so we are sure to grab the right size when mixing. We have the standard jigger mentioned above, the ¾ ounce, ½ ounce, 1¼ ounce, and 2 ounce.

Garnishes. Lemon and lime are the most commonly used garnishes. Having these handy is great because you can use the juice for mixing, and the leftovers for garnishes. Big olives are also a good idea to have because they have a long shelf life and go great with a variety of cocktails. You'll notice we have a wide array of garnishes on our cocktails. You can throw every f*cking edible thing in your refrigerator on something like a bloody mary, but we want you to have the basics. If all else fails, squeeze a bunch of citrus on some booze and call it a day.

Modifiers. There are countless mixers and drink modifiers, but the three most important and common are tonic, soda water, and simple syrup. Simple syrup is 1 cup water and 1 cup sugar. You can easily make your own simple syrup; use a sugar alternative if you prefer. After you have those, look for Cointreau, vermouth, and bitters. Bitters is used sparingly, and the shelf life is long, so just pick up a small bottle and know it will last you a while. And remember, the components of a balanced cocktail are alcohol, sweet, bitter, and sour.

ALCOHOL! Booze is what this book is all about. If you're on a budget, start with a bottle of vodka and a bottle of tequila. They are the most versatile. From there, stock your bar with white rum, gin, and whiskey.

Glassware. There are so many different types of glassware, you will be overwhelmed if you try to buy every different option you see in the recipes. Start with the three basics: a tall glass, a short glass (also known as a rocks glass), and a stemmed glass. You can drink our cocktails out of a f*cking shoe if you're desperate, so don't feel like it is necessary to pick up any new glassware. However, if you're having a dinner party and want your cocktails to look their best, you'll have to invest in some. You'll also want to pick up some shot glasses. Most people get shot glasses as a souvenir, so you may have a Britney one handy from her Vegas residency, or a Grand Canyon one from a family trip. We recommend buying some unbranded shot glasses for special guests, and you can set aside that Britney one for a *very* special guest. For wine, there are different glasses for different varietals, but if you have limited space or money, stick to one style of wine glass that is in between so you can serve whatever you uncork/unscrew in them. Moscow mule mugs look great on your bar, but you may not use them often.

All of these are suggestions. You can pick up some cheap disposable (recyclable) cups at the drugstore if you don't have the room for storing extra glassware. You can also pick up a lot of great glassware at thrift shops. We've gotten tea sets from Goodwill for $10. Thrift store finds are unique and make it easy to ball on a budget.

The most important thing to keep in mind when you're reading this book is that we want you to have fun. Don't feel like you have to go out and spend a bunch of money to make these. Everything is customizable. Don't have a martini glass? Serve it in a paper cup. A recipe may call for blood orange juice, but you may only be able to find regular OJ. That's *good as gold*! These recipes were carefully crafted to be the best they can be, but shit happens, and you may need to adjust. Or try a different recipe based on the ingredients you have. We included some drinks that call for ingredients that you may have to order online or at a high-end liquor store, and there are other drinks you can make with the sauce packets you have from the drive-thru and an empty water bottle. Have fun and *get loose*! And if you're not having fun, drink until you *are* having fun.

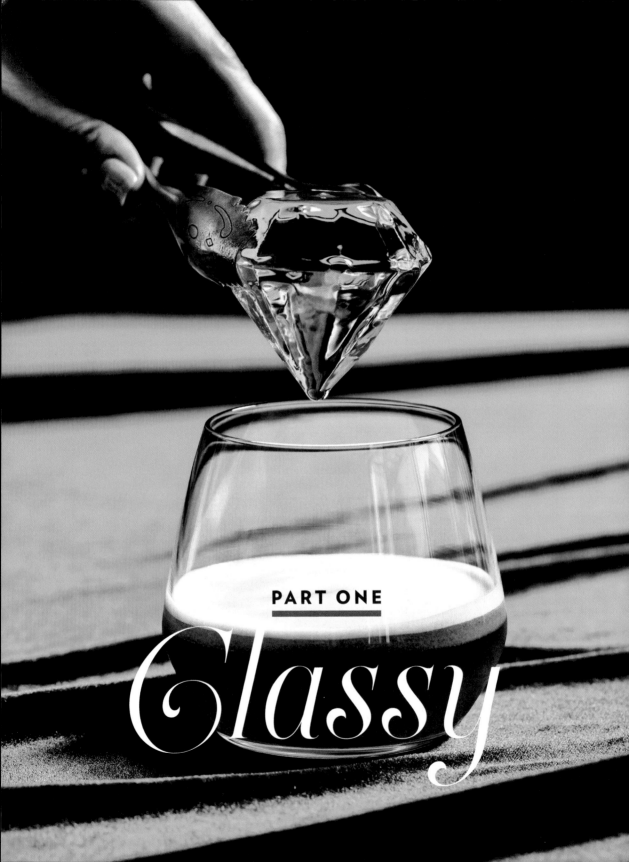

PART ONE

Classy

THE
Cosmo

ARIANA ❖ This is a recipe we made on the show when I was new to SUR. Jax, Tom, and I had a contest for who could make the best SUR Cosmo. I won, despite Tom being the one who trained me to make it. Tom ultimately didn't put enough sweetener in the mix. Depending on the liquor you use, you may find yourself needing a little more fruit juice to balance out the cocktail. I personally like less sugar, but when I'm working with vodka, I know I need some balance. *Serves 1*

GLASSWARE

4 lime wedges

¼ ounce simple syrup (see below)

2½ ounces vodka

Splash cranberry juice

In a cocktail shaker, muddle the lime wedges. Continue to muddle while adding the simple syrup, vodka, and a splash of cranberry juice for color. Fill the cocktail shaker to the top with ice. Shake. Strain into a martini glass.

MARTINI GLASS

Note

When the liquids are combined in the cocktail shaker with ice, you want to shake it right away. The more you shake, the more watered-down your final cocktail will be.

SPECIAL TOOLS

Cocktail Shaker

❋

Muddler

HOMEMADE SIMPLE SYRUP

1 cup water ❖ **1 cup sugar**

In saucepan, heat the water and sugar until boiling. Remove from the heat. Stir until sugar dissolves. Allow to cool.

NOTE: Replace the sugar with your desired sugar alternative if you prefer another sweetener. If replacing with Splenda, the ratio will stay the same, but you may need to add more or less if using something else.

SPIRIT

VODKA

MARGARITAS

ARIANA & TOM • Everyone loves a margarita.
In my experience, they can be done poorly. I'm sure you've all had
one that had way too much sour mix. It's important to balance.
We created a variety of margaritas for this book so you
can choose the one that's right for you.

2

4

5

STL Red Hot
Rita

TOM * I love St. Louis! I grew up there, and try to make it back as much as I can. Even though I left when I was eighteen and now live in LA, I will always call St. Louis home. Nothing beats going to a Cards game in the summer. Growing up, I couldn't have had better or more hardworking parents. My dad worked two full-time jobs in the same building. My mom is a retired firefighter, and in 1997 was the first woman to be awarded "Firefighter of the Year" in St. Louis County. I'm so proud of what she did for the city. They're both my heroes and all-around badasses. Wherever life takes me, I will never forget where I came from. This drink is dedicated to Andy Cohen, the Blues, the Cardinals, the best damn sports fans, and my awesome family and friends back home. #PlayGloria ***Serves 1***

DRINK RATING

TRASHY   CLASSY

GLASSWARE

MARGARITA GLASS

SPECIAL TOOL

Cocktail Shaker

SPIRITS

TEQUILA
COINTREAU
BUD LIGHT BEER

1 lime wedge

Red Hot Riplets seasoning

1½ ounces spicy tequila (see note)

½ ounce Cointreau

¾ ounce strawberry puree (page 105)

½ ounce lime juice

½ ounce sour mix (page 22)

1 can Bud Light beer

Dampen the rim of the glass with a lime wedge. Dip the rim into Red Hot Riplets seasoning.

Pour the spicy tequila, Cointreau, strawberry puree, lime juice, and sour mix into a cocktail shaker. Fill the remainder of the cocktail shaker with ice. Shake and strain over fresh crushed ice into the rimmed margarita glass.

Top with 1 can of Bud Light and dash of Red Hot Riplets.

Note

Make the margarita skinny-style by subbing the sour mix with more fresh lime juice. You can also purchase sour mix, but homemade always tastes better! For spicy tequila, soak peppers of choice in a bottle of tequila overnight. If you want it spicier, soak longer.

CONTINUES

1 cup sugar ◆ **1 cup water** ◆ **½ cup lime juice** ◆ **½ cup lemon juice**

In a saucepan, bring the sugar and water to a boil. Remove from the heat. Stir until the sugar dissolves. Add the lemon and lime juice and stir.

Berry
MARGARITA

ARIANA ⟶ The Berry Margarita is my favorite. Blackberries give it a great color, and it's perfect for drinking on the sand or in your backyard on a summer day. *Serves 1*

3 lime wedges

Salt

3 fresh basil leaves

3 blackberries

½ ounce light agave nectar

1½ ounces blanco tequila

½ ounce Cointreau

Garnish: Blackberry, fresh basil leaf

Using a lime wedge, dampen the rim of the glass. Dip the rim in salt.

Muddle all three lime wedges, the basil leaves, blackberries, and agave nectar in a cocktail shaker. Fill the remainder of the cocktail shaker with ice. Add the tequila and Cointreau. Shake well. Strain into the salted glass over fresh ice.

Garnish with blackberry and basil leaf.

Note

If blackberries are out of season, try blueberries or raspberries. Hell, you can even combine all three of them.

DRINK RATING

TRASHY   CLASSY

GLASSWARE

SHORT GLASS

SPECIAL TOOL

Cocktail Shaker

SPIRITS

BLANCO TEQUILA

COINTREAU

Cucumber Pomegranate

MARGARITA

TOM » Cucumber and pomegranate go together beautifully. You'll often find them paired in a salad, but you can also combine them in drink form. *Serves 1*

10 to 15 pomegranate seeds (or use pomegranate juice)

¼ ounce cardamom syrup

2 ounces blanco tequila

1 ounce cucumber juice

¾ ounce lime juice

Garnish: Cucumber slice, pomegranate seeds

In a cocktail shaker, muddle the pomegranate seeds with the cardamom syrup. Fill the remainder of the cocktail shaker with ice. Add the tequila, cucumber juice, and lime juice. Shake and strain into a glass over fresh ice.

Garnish with a cucumber slice, pomegranate seeds, or both.

DRINK RATING

TRASHY   CLASSY

GLASSWARE

SHORT GLASS

SPECIAL TOOLS

Cocktail Shaker

✳

Muddler

SPIRIT

BLANCO TEQUILA

GLASSWARE

SHORT GLASS

SPECIAL TOOL

Cocktail Shaker

SPIRIT

BLANCO TEQUILA

Blood Orange
MARGARITA

ARIANA ☀ We use a lot of blood oranges in our cocktails because they add a different flavor than sweet oranges. They are also great for garnishing because they are orange on the outside and have a pink, red, or purple coloring on the inside. *Serves 1*

2 ounces blanco tequila

1 ounce lime juice

1 ounce blood orange juice

½ ounce agave nectar

Garnish: Blood orange slice

Add the tequila, lime juice, blood orange juice, and agave nectar to a cocktail shaker. Fill the remainder of the cocktail shaker with ice. Shake and strain into a glass over fresh ice.

Garnish with blood orange slice.

Note

People always order a "skinny" margarita without knowing exactly what that means for the ingredients. *Skinny* means the cocktail has a natural sweetener like lime juice or agave nectar, and none of that slushy, syrupy sweet-and-sour mix. Most bars have moved away from the artificial mix that was so popular in the 90s, so if you go to a reputable establishment, you can typically order a margarita without having to specify "skinny."

Classic Marg

ARIANA → Sometimes you just want a simple margarita. No bells, no whistles, just a salted rim and tequila base. *Serves 1*

1 lime wedge

Salt

2 lemon wedges

½ ounce light agave nectar

2 ounces blanco tequila

½ ounce Cointreau

Garnish: Lime wedge

Using a lime wedge, dampen the rim of the glass. Dip the rim in salt.

In a cocktail shaker, muddle the lime and lemon wedges into the agave nectar. Fill the remainder of the cocktail shaker with ice. Add the tequila and Cointreau. Shake and strain into a glass over fresh ice.

Garnish with the remaining lime wedge.

Note

If you're on the fence about salting your glass, just salt half. That way there's no commitment.

GLASSWARE

SHORT GLASS

SPECIAL TOOL

Cocktail Shaker

Muddler

SPIRITS

BLANCO TEQUILA

COINTREAU

TRASHY   CLASSY

GLASSWARE

SHORT GLASS

SPECIAL TOOLS

Cocktail Shaker

✽

Muddler

SPIRIT

BOURBON

Mint Jewel

ARIANA ⚹ I've always loved going to the Kentucky Derby. A Derby staple is the mint julep. I find that juleps are made either too sweet or without enough mint. It's a simple drink, but sometimes the simplest cocktails can be the ones that are most easily ruined. There's nothing worse than taking two sips of a drink and then spilling it out. *Serves 1*

10 fresh mint sprigs

2½ ounces bourbon

½ ounce simple syrup (page 17)

Garnish: Lemon zest, fresh mint sprig, powdered sugar

In a cocktail shaker, muddle the mint sprigs to release the aroma. Add the bourbon and simple syrup. Fill the remainder of the cocktail shaker with ice. Stir, don't shake. Pour contents into a short glass over fresh ice.

Garnish with lemon zest, mint sprig, and a sprinkle of powdered sugar.

Note

Powdered sugar and confectioners' sugar are the same. Look for either in your grocery store.

Ghost of Mary

TOM ⟶ We call this the Ghost of Mary because it's infused with ghost pepper and it looks like the ghost of a former Bloody Mary. This is a drink that you need to make ahead of time. You can't just pull it out of your ass. You need freezer time, but the extra prep will be worth it in the end, since all of the flavors get the chance to infuse with each other. The final tomato garnish will impress your guests, but if you're not comfortable working with fire, be sure to skip that step. You don't want to burn your place down trying to look cool. *Serves 1*

Chili powder

Salt

1 lemon wedge

1½ ounces vodka

½ ounce aquavit

2½ ounces ghost mix (page 32)

Garnish: 1 mozzarella ball, fresh rosemary sprig, 1 tomato (optional), 1 teaspoon absinthe (optional)

Mix chili powder and salt to make the rimming salt. Dampen the rim of glass with the lemon wedge. Dip the rim of the glass into the salt mixture.

Add the vodka, aquavit, and ghost mix to a cocktail shaker and shake until well-blended. Pour over ice in the rimmed glass.

Garnish with the mozzarella ball and sprig of rosemary. If you're feeling extra spicy, dip a tomato into absinthe, then add to the drink garnish and carefully light the tomato on fire upon serving.

GLASSWARE

COLLINS GLASS

SPECIAL TOOLS

Cocktail Shaker

❋

Strainer

❋

Lighter (optional)

SPIRITS

VODKA

AQUAVIT

CONTINUES

Note

If you want to save some time, you can sub in your favorite premade
Bloody Mary mix. If you want to purchase a premade mix, be sure to look for one
without a lot of preservatives and sugar. Our Ghost Mix is clear, so just note
that a premade one will change the coloring of the cocktail. Also, those
loaded-with-chemicals mixes sometimes make your drinks taste like liquid chalk.

GHOST MIX

3 pounds yellow and green heirloom tomatoes • ½ pound white onion •
1 ounce lemon juice • 1 clove garlic, minced • 1 teaspoon Himalayan sea salt
• 1 teaspoon black pepper • ½ teaspoon Old Bay Seasoning •
2 dried basil leaves, chopped • 4 ounces arugula • 1 stalk celery •
1 serrano pepper • ½ teaspoon ghost pepper powder • Dash bitters

Combine all ingredients in a blender and puree. Pour
the contents into a bowl and freeze overnight. Take out the frozen block
and wrap it in cheesecloth. Suspend the cheesecloth over a large bowl
in a strainer or tied to a wooden spoon. Strain overnight. The tomato-
flavored liquid that is left will be your Bloody Mary base.

Rosy Disposition

ARIANA ⟶ This drink is our ode to Scheana. Scheana is kindhearted and positive, and it often feels like she looks at life through rose-colored glasses. The first episode of *Vanderpump Rules* opened with Scheana having a conversation with Brandi from *The Real Housewives of Beverly Hills*. She had previously worked at Villa Blanca, which is where I met her a few years before, but she made the transition into SUR and became the audience surrogate. When the other cast members were telling Scheana "this is what it's like to work here," they were really telling the audience at home. I did not think we would be close, but we bonded over exes and video games, and have been friends ever since. #ItsAllHappening. *Serves 1*

¾ **ounce lemon juice**

3 strawberries

¾ **ounce simple syrup (page 17)**

2 dashes rose water (page 34; see note)

2 ounces vodka

½ **ounce Champagne**

Garnish: Rose petals, strawberries

In a cocktail shaker, muddle the lemon juice, strawberries, and simple syrup. Add 2 dashes of rose water and vodka. Fill the remainder of the cocktail shaker with ice. Shake and strain into a glass over fresh ice. Top with the Champagne.

Garnish with rose petals and strawberries.

Note

You don't have to make your own rose water; many stores carry it.

CONTINUES

HOMEMADE ROSE WATER

¹/₂ cup fresh rose petals ◆ 1¹/₂ cups water

Wash any residue off the rose petals. In a saucepan, heat the rose petals and water. Cover and bring to a boil. Reduce the heat to low. Simmer until the petals lose coloring, approximately 10 minutes. Strain.

NOTE: Rose water lasts several weeks in refrigerator.

Pinky's Lemonade

ARIANA ⚬ This is a summer drink, which I created on one of the hottest summer days in recent memory. My car was without air conditioning at the time, I needed a drink, and it needed to be something refreshing. This may sound like a lot of flavors, but they all mix well—perfect for the hot sun or sipping poolside. After I made it, Lisa tried it and wanted to sell it at SUR for Pride. I named it as an homage to her (Lisa's nickname is Pinky). *Serves 1*

3 fresh basil leaves

3 lemon wedges

1½ ounces vodka

3 ounces LVP Pink Sangria

Splash club soda

Garnish: Lemon zest, fresh basil leaves

In a cocktail shaker, muddle the basil and lemon wedges. Add the vodka and pink sangria. Fill the remainder of the cocktail shaker with ice. Shake and strain into a tall glass. Add fresh ice and top with a splash of club soda.

Garnish with the lemon zest and basil leaves.

Note

You don't always have to strain your drinks when you're using a cocktail shaker. This is one of those that can go either way. If you like having bits of lemon in your drink, forgo the fresh ice and serve direct from the cocktail shaker into a fresh glass.

DRINK RATING

TRASHY   CLASSY

GLASSWARE

TALL GLASS

SPECIAL TOOLS

Cocktail Shaker

❋

Muddler

SPIRITS

VODKA

LVP PINK SANGRIA

GLASSWARE

ROCKS GLASS

SPECIAL TOOLS

Cocktail Shaker

✳

Muddler

SPIRIT

VODKA

Cape Canaveral Caprese

ARIANA ✳ Whenever I order a martini, I ask for extra olives. It's nice to have a little snack while you're drinking. The Cape Canaveral Caprese takes that idea one step farther. It's more than a drink: It's an appetizer. If you're having a dinner party, surprise your guests by serving this during cocktail hour. The unexpected flavors will surprise them, and it's the perfect warm-up to the main course. The name, of course, is in reference to where I'm from. I've been in Los Angeles for years now, but I'm originally from Florida. I was born during a meteor shower, and I've watched space shuttle launches from the front yard my whole life. I still think I see meteor showers and shooting stars more than the average person. *Serves 1*

3 fresh basil leaves

3 heirloom cherry tomatoes

¾ ounce simple syrup (page 17)

1½ ounces vodka

¼ ounce balsamic vinegar

Garnish: Skewer of fresh basil leaf, tomato, and a mozzarella ball, cracked pepper

In a cocktail shaker, muddle the basil leaves and cherry tomatoes with the simple syrup. Fill the remainder of the shaker with ice. Add the vodka and vinegar. Shake and strain over ice.

Garnish with a skewer of basil, tomato, and a mozzarella ball. Finish with cracked pepper on top.

Note

The skewer garnish is an appetizer in and of itself. When serving, instead of putting the skewer in the drink upright, lay it across the rim of the glass. The person drinking can decide if they want to dip the tomato, basil, and mozzarella in the cocktail, or eat it and then chase it with the booze.

Red Devil

TOM ⁕ It's important to always name your drink. Naming it gives
it an identity. It makes the cocktail unique and, most importantly,
memorable. Before my SUR days, I was bartending a private party at
a prominent agent's house. There were no signature drinks to serve
because the bar was limited. People were mainly asking for vodka
sodas. That is, until the Material Girl herself walked up to the bar. She
looked apprehensive, so I took control of the situation and asked her
if she would like to try a Red Devil. She said "okay," intrigued by the
name I gave it. I quickly turned, threw something together, and made
sure it was RED! She took a sip, her face lit up, and she smiled and coyly
walked away. It ended up being a version of the following recipe, and it
was a hit. I was making Red Devils for A-listers the rest of the night.
I've since perfected the cocktail, but I'll always remember the first time
I served it to the Queen of Pop.

    ARIANA ⁕ Tom, of course, told me the Red Devil story. The first
time I had it . . . I was feeling bad and I couldn't explain. My soul was
there, my hips were moving at a rapid pace . . . I lied, that's just lyrics
(sorta) from Madonna and Britney's "Me Against the Music." Couldn't
pass up the opportunity to quote the infamous collab. *Serves 1*

2 ounces black currant vodka

½ ounce tangerine juice (see note)

½ ounce Grand Marnier

¾ ounce pomegranate juice

½ ounce bitters

Splash of soda

Garnish: Red pepper slice, lime wedge

In a cocktail shaker, stir together
the vodka, tangerine juice, Grand
Marnier, juice, and bitters. Add a
splash of soda. Pour over ice in a
rocks glass.

    Garnish with red pepper
slice. Squeeze a lime wedge on
top.

Note

If you don't have tangerine juice, replace with orange juice.

DRINK RATING

TRASHY   CLASSY

GLASSWARE

**ROCKS
GLASS**

SPECIAL TOOL

Cocktail Shaker

SPIRITS

BLACK CURRANT
VODKA

GRAND MARNIER

GLASSWARE

MARTINI GLASS

SPECIAL TOOL

Cocktail Shaker

SPIRITS

CLEAR WHISKEY

CLEAR SWEET VERMOUTH

ALOE LIQUEUR

Going Clear

TOM ❋ Going Clear looks and feels purely elegant. It is a reference to exposing the truth, but it literally is a clear Manhattan. Sandoval Surgeon General's Warning: the more of these you drink, the more truth you may expose. Secrets could get leaked, scandals could be unleashed, and emotional storms could rage. You have been warned. ***Serves 1***

2 ounces clear whiskey

¾ ounce clear sweet vermouth

½ ounce aloe liqueur

Pour the whiskey, vermouth, and aloe liqueur into a cocktail shaker. Fill the remainder of the cocktail shaker with ice. Stir. Strain into a martini glass.

Note

This drink is clear, so be sure to use a clear whiskey and clear sweet vermouth.

PASSIONFRUIT PUREE

To make the puree, cut *1 passionfruit* in half cross-wise.
Scoop out seeds and pulp. Combine the pulp of the passionfruit in a
blender with *2 ounces water* and *2 ounces granulated Splenda*.
Blend until smooth and chill until needed.

SHIBUYA
Crossing

ARIANA ✳ People who watch *Vanderpump Rules* are often surprised when they see us out together without cameras. The truth is, we are all actually friends IRL. We don't *just* vacation together with a camera crew in tow. Recently, Tom and I went to Japan with Katie and Schwartz. We had the most amazing time trying the local food and cocktails. Traveling with them is great because Katie is very organized and the four of us can (usually) get along with little-to-no drama between us. We spent a lot of time in a little dive bar near our hotel and we fell in love with the infused rums and Japanese whiskey. We also fell in love with Shibuya Crossing, where we did some Mario-style kart racing. If you're having some friends over for a Japanese-inspired dinner, this drink will go perfectly with the meal. It's elegant and delicious. *Serves 1*

3 shiso leaves

¾ ounce lemon juice

¾ ounce ginger syrup

¾ ounce passionfruit puree (see opposite)

1½ ounces wasabi-infused white rum

½ ounce Japanese whiskey

Crushed ice for serving

Ginger beer

Garnish: Green or purple shiso leaves

In a cocktail shaker, muddle two of the shiso leaves. Pour in the lemon juice, ginger syrup, passionfruit puree, rum, and whiskey and fill the remainder of the shaker with ice. Shake and strain into a glass over fresh crushed ice, then top with ginger beer.

Garnish with green or purple shiso leaves.

Note

Infusing spirits yourself is great, because over time you can cater the infusion to your liking. For instance, if you like spicy and you're infusing with peppers, add more peppers. For the ginger syrup in this drink, you can make your own using *wasanbon* (Japanese sugar).

GLASSWARE

TALL GLASS

SPECIAL TOOLS

Cocktail Shaker

✳

Muddler

SPIRITS

WASABI-INFUSED WHITE RUM

JAPANESE WHISKEY

GLASSWARE

MARTINI GLASS

SPECIAL TOOLS

Cocktail Shaker

❋

Santa Hat

SPIRITS

CHOCOLATE LIQUEUR

CHILI CHOCOLATE
KAHLÚA

VANILLA VODKA

NAUGHTY
Holiday

TOM ❋ Ariana and I often get asked to do press together, since we're one of the resident couples on the show. One of the networks asked us to do a segment for a show around the holidays. We decided it would be fun to make competing recipes. Both of them turned out great (her Nice Holiday recipe can be found on page 49). Whether you're throwing a Christmas party, or just boozing solo while you listen to a classic like "Sleigh Ride," this is the perfect accompaniment to your festivities. My Naughty Holiday recipe is a little different than Ariana's Nice Holiday recipe in that it is a bit spicier. The holidays can be sad AF, but being gluttonous with alcohol can help. ***Serves 1***

1½ ounces chocolate liqueur

1½ ounces Chili Chocolate Kahlúa

1½ ounce vanilla vodka

Chili powder

Garnish: Dark chocolate shavings, red pepper

Put the chocolate liqueur, Kahlúa, and vodka into a cocktail shaker. Fill the remainder with ice. Shake and strain into a martini glass.

Top with a dash of chili powder, and garnish with the dark chocolate shavings and red pepper.

Note

Garnishes are great for spicing up holiday drinks. You can alter most of the recipes in this book and add a candy cane or cinnamon stick if you're serving it in November or December. Cranberries, pomegranates, cherries, and strawberries can also give you that beautiful holiday red, and if you're looking for a deep green, try mixing one of those fruits with an herb like fresh rosemary, basil, or thyme.

Nice Holiday

ARIANA * The Nice Holiday is extra indulgent. Pop on Mariah Carey's "All I Want for Christmas is You!" and enjoy by the fire with a loved one. *Serves 1*

2 ounces white chocolate liqueur

½ ounce crème de menthe

1 ounce vanilla vodka

Garnish: Whipped cream, chocolate mints, fresh mint leaf

Add all ingredients (except the garnish) to a cocktail shaker. Fill with ice. Shake and strain into a chilled martini glass.

Garnish with whipped cream, chocolate mints, and a fresh mint leaf.

Note

You can get as gluttonous as you want with the garnish on this one. The holidays are a time to eat, so put your favorite chocolate mints on top, or hang a candy cane off the rim. This also tastes best cold, so be sure to use a chilled martini glass and keep the whipped cream as cold as possible before serving.

TRASHY   CLASSY

GLASSWARE

TALL GLASS

SPECIAL TOOLS

Cocktail Shaker

❋

Muddler

SPIRIT

SAKE

Sake Mojito

ARIANA ❋ Mojitos always remind me of a Vegas pool drink. It's an easy drink to make, plus it's light and flavorful, not too heavy to drink under the hot sun by a pool. There isn't much more to it than something like a vodka soda, but it FEELS a little fancier, you know what I mean? It's just a few simple ingredients that most people have on hand. I like to sub sake for the usual rum. Both are great, and the most important aspect of a mojito is the lime and mint mixture. *Serves 1*

3 lime wedges

3 fresh mint leaves

½ ounce simple syrup (page 17)

3 ounces sake

Club soda

Garnish: Sprig of fresh mint, edible flowers

In a cocktail shaker, muddle the lime wedges and mint leaves with the simple syrup. Fill the remainder of the shaker with ice. Add the sake. Shake and strain into a tall glass over fresh ice. Top with club soda.

Garnish with a sprig of fresh mint and edible flowers.

Note

A traditional mojito is made with white rum. Substitute for the sake if you're looking for a classic mojito.

Peach Pit

ARIANA AND TOM → TomTom and SUR are our Peach Pit. If any of you grew up watching *90210*, you know that the Peach Pit was the cast hangout. Eventually Steve had the idea for After Dark, and Dylan bought the building and opened Peach Pit After Dark, which was later owned by Valerie Malone after she . . . never mind. The point, is SUR is our Peach Pit. Or for *Saved by the Bell* fans, it's our Max. Or if you grew up loving *Friends*, it's our Central Perk. It's our Luke's Diner, Monk's Café, Chubbie's Famous, and Krusty Krab. It's our spot. This recipe calls for peach pecan whiskey, which is delicious. You can enjoy this with your friends at your own hangout spot, or at home while you're watching your favorite shows. ***Serves 1***

2 strawberries

¾ ounce lemon juice

Dash of ground cinnamon

2 ounces peach pecan whiskey

¼ ounce agave nectar

½ ounce water

5 drops almond extract

Dash of bitters (optional)

Garnish: *Maple leaf*

In a cocktail shaker, muddle the strawberries with the lemon juice and cinnamon. Add the whiskey, agave nectar, water, almond extract, and bitters. Fill the remainder of the shaker with ice. Shake and strain into a martini glass.

Garnish with the maple leaf.

Note

This is a great Thanksgiving drink. The cinnamon and almond flavors will go great with a pumpkin or sweet potato pie. For an extra holiday touch, garnish with a cinnamon stick.

DRINK RATING

TRASHY   CLASSY

GLASSWARE

MARTINI GLASS

SPECIAL TOOLS

Cocktail Shaker

❋

Muddler

SPIRIT

PEACH PECAN WHISKEY

GLASSWARE

COUPE GLASS

SPECIAL TOOLS

Cocktail Shaker

✳

Muddler

SPIRIT

REPOSADO TEQUILA

Doc Holliday

TOM ✳ *Tombstone* is one of my favorite movies. Val Kilmer plays Doc Holliday in the flick. One Halloween, Schwartz and I had a costume party to go to and I decided to dress up as Doc. I learned to sideways twirl cast-iron cap guns to further commit to my costume. Schwartz videotaped me doing my newly learned party trick. A few months later, Labrinth was casting for their new music video for "Express Yourself." They needed someone who could do some gun tricks, so I submitted the video of me playing around with my toy guns. They cast me based off that Halloween clip. The video is online and you can see me working my magic for a few seconds in the final product. I set out to make a cocktail that was an homage to *Tombstone* and the Wild West. This drink has the savory and the sweet. I like to think the red pepper battles the mint for dominance but, in the end, the guava and lime bring them together and they get married and ride off with the tequila into the sunset. *Serves 1*

2 slices of red pepper

5 fresh mint leaves

½ ounce simple syrup (page 17)

1¼ ounces lime juice

2 ounces reposado tequila

¾ ounce guava juice

Garnish: Fresh mint leaf, red pepper slice

In a cocktail shaker, muddle the red pepper and 4 mint leaves with the simple syrup. Add the lime juice, tequila, and guava juice. Fill the remainder of shaker with ice. Shake and strain into a coupe glass (see note).

Garnish with remaining mint leaf and red pepper slice.

Note

Coupe glasses aren't as common as martini glasses. The Doc Holliday looks best in a coupe, but feel free to use a martini if that's all you have. Hell, you can use a Solo cup if that's all you have. We don't judge.

Gossamer

ARIANA ⁎ The Gossamer is a cocktail that is perfect for a late-summer day drink. It's a mix of summer and fall flavors, so pour a glass and plan your Halloween costume, or guzzle it up while you reminisce about your favorite summer moments. ***Serves 1***

1¼ ounces cantaloupe (roughly 4 melon balls)

1¼ ounces vanilla vodka

¼ ounce cinnamon-infused agave nectar

Champagne

Garnish: Ground cinnamon, melon ball

In a cocktail shaker, muddle the cantaloupe with the agave nectar. Add the vodka. Fill the remainder of the shaker with ice. Shake and strain over fresh ice. Top with Champagne.

Garnish with the cinnamon and a melon ball.

Note

Don't open a nice bottle of Champagne to top if you're only serving one. The Champagne will add a nice fizz to top the cocktail, but it's expensive and will go to waste if you aren't making a few of them. We recommend starting your morning with mimosas and transitioning into Gossamers in the afternoon. Use your leftover mimosa Champagne for your topper.

DRINK RATING

TRASHY   CLASSY

GLASSWARE

ROCKS GLASS

SPECIAL TOOLS

Melon Baller

✳

Cocktail Shaker

✳

Muddler

SPIRITS

VANILLA VODKA

CHAMPAGNE

ALCHEMY
Rose

TOM → Schwartz and I created this in his kitchen. A version of it is on the menu at TomTom. Before we opened, we worked for months trying to create the perfect cocktails. We would go to the liquor store and buy the craziest ingredients we could find. It was important to us that the drinks on the menu are unique and special. Tom and I would put on music and mix it all: spices, fruits, anything we could find. We must've made 50 to 60 drinks in preparation. It has been so gratifying to see TomTom open and thriving, but it was even more fun prepping the cocktails with my best friend. *Serves 1*

1½ ounces gin

½ ounce ginger liqueur

¾ ounce hibiscus syrup (see note)

¾ ounce lemon juice

½ ounce aquafaba (below)

Garnish: Dried hibiscus flower

In a chilled coupe glass, mix the gin, liqueur, syrup, lemon juice, and aquafaba. Stir.

Garnish with dried hibiscus flower.

Note

You can buy hibiscus syrup ready-made, or make your own. It's basically hibiscus-infused simple syrup, so you just need sugar, water, and hibiscus flowers.

AQUAFABA

Use this as a substitute for whipped egg whites in most recipes.

1 can chickpeas

Drain a can of chickpeas and reserve the liquid. In a small bowl, whip the reserved liquid using a hand mixer until firm peaks form, 3 to 5 minutes. You can whip by hand, but it will take some time to get it to the right consistency.

GLASSWARE

COUPE
GLASS

SPIRIT

GIN

GINGER LIQUEUR

FTB

TOM ❖ FTB stands for "Fear the Boss." On *Vanderpump Rules* we always fear the boss. The FTB was one of those cocktails that Schwartz and I crafted for TomTom. Initially, Schwartz wanted to do a jalapeño-infused agave nectar. He thought it would be spicy enough, but I knew it would get diluted once it was mixed. Before even serving it to Lisa, I was nervous she would think it wasn't spicy enough. I feared the boss. Turns out I was right, and it needed an extra kick. We added the jalapeño slices to give it the oomph it needed and it turned out perfect. *Serves 1*

⅓ ounce light agave nectar

3 jalapeño slices

2 ounces mezcal

¾ lemon juice

½ ounce prickly pear juice

½ ounce aquafaba (page 58)

In a cocktail shaker, muddle the agave nectar and jalapeño slices. Add the mezcal, lemon juice, prickly pear juice, and aquafaba. Fill the remainder of the shaker with ice. Shake and strain over fresh ice in a rocks glass.

Note

Fresh jalapeños work best, but you can use canned or jarred peppers if that's all you have. (Just don't use pickled.) If you're working with fresh, be sure to wear gloves and wash your hands thoroughly after using. You don't want jalapeño dick because you were careless with the jalapeño before going to the bathroom.

DRINK RATING

TRASHY   CLASSY

GLASSWARE

ROCKS GLASS

SPECIAL TOOLS

Cocktail Shaker

❋

Muddler

SPIRIT

MEZCAL

TH Tea

GLASSWARE

ROCKS GLASS

SPECIAL TOOLS

Cocktail Shaker

❋

Eyedropper

SPIRIT

GIN

GREEN TEA LIQUEUR

GINGER LIQUEUR

ARIANA ❋ Remember in the *Sex and the City* movie when Carrie was in her "Mexicoma"? She was sad that Big doubted the wedding, and she found herself on her honeymoon vacation with her girlfriends. Eventually, Charlotte Poughkeepsied in her pants and snapped Carrie out of her Mexicoma. I had an experience like that a few years back. I snuck some weed into a music festival by stuffing it into a tampon applicator. I had never done that before, but it seemed like a great way to get it into the venue. When my friend Jenna and I got to the festival, there was lots of marijuana being passed around, so I didn't need to dig into my purse. My dad passed shortly after the festival, and life stopped as I went home for his memorial. During the services, I excused myself to the bathroom because it was that time of the month. I went into my purse for a tampon and saw the weed-filled applicator. I started laughing hysterically. I snapped out of my Mexicoma. My friend Danny always says, "On the other side of a bad day is a smile." The smiles may not come when you need them, but they will come eventually. *Serves 1*

1 ounce gin

¾ ounce green tea liqueur

½ ounce ginger liqueur

¾ ounce lemon juice

½ teaspoon matcha powder

⅓ ounce ginger-infused agave nectar

Kombucha (see note)

15 mg CBD oil (2 to 3 drops; see note)

Into a cocktail shaker, put the gin, liqueurs, lemon juice, matcha, and agave. Fill the remainder of the shaker with ice. Shake and strain over fresh ice. Top with kombucha.

Using an eyedropper, add 2 to 3 drops of CBD oil.

Note

Mint-lemonade kombucha is a great topper to this cocktail, but you might not have that handy or readily available at your local grocery. Use whatever flavor kombucha you prefer.

When it comes to CBD, you can use oil or tincture. The oil will rise to the top. This allows the person drinking to see the oil and smell it before they drink it. Tincture mixes better.

BLIND I

One of our castmates
weed tea before conf
is until she accident
some kief that gave
She was so stoned w
at the studio, produc
another cast memb
and film in her place.
purple floor and

A Little Muddy

ARIANA → Whenever I go to a chain restaurant, I salivate over their dessert drinks. You know, the ones that throw all sorts of shit in a blender and then top with liquor and serve with blooming onion deliciousness? I don't know about you, but every time I have one of those drinks, I end up feeling gross. This recipe is my take on that. It's not *too* much, so you can have more than one. It's a healthy-ish mudslide. **Serves 1**

1 ounce vodka

½ ounce banana rum

½ ounce coffee-flavored liqueur

1 ounce almond milk

¼ teaspoon maca powder

¼ teaspoon chai tea powder

¼ ounce date syrup

¼ ounce aquafaba (page 58)

1 cup ice

Garnish: Blueberries or a cherry

In a blender, put the vodka, banana rum, coffee-flavored liqueur, almond milk, maca powder, chai tea powder, date syrup, and aquafaba. Add the 1 cup ice. Blend. Pour into a milkshake glass.

Garnish with blueberries or a cherry.

Note

If you don't mind adding some calories, garnish with whipped cream, a drizzle of chocolate syrup, *and* a cherry. That will really give it the mudslide vibe.

DRINK RATING

TRASHY   CLASSY

GLASSWARE

MILKSHAKE GLASS

SPECIAL TOOL

Blender

SPIRITS

VODKA

BANANA RUM

COFFEE-FLAVORED LIQUEUR

Sidecar

TOM → Opening TomTom was a huge accomplishment for me. About a year before we opened, I started to think of ways Tom Schwartz and I could make our entrance. I knew it had to be big and cinematic. As the opening got closer, I had the idea of riding up to the front doors of TomTom in a motorcycle with a sidecar. Initially, I looked into renting one, but I couldn't find anything. I eventually bought one in Miami. I wanted it to be a surprise for Tom, so I wasn't able to pick it up myself. My friend Memo was able to make the trip for me. Once I saw it in person, I knew it needed lots of work. Not only was it not starting, but it needed a complete overhaul. Thunder Road is a great company nearby, and I left it in their very capable hands.

When it was finally time to roll, I got all dressed up and went to pick up the bike. It turns out that the sidecar is harder to attach than I anticipated. Luckily there was a barista nearby who was able to help Thunder Road and me attach the sidecar. Now keep in mind I got on the motorcycle around 4 o'clock. I was already supposed to be at Schwartz's house to pick him up. Tom thought I was picking him up in a car, but I arrived in this freshly painted bike. He loves the movie *Varsity Blues*, so I played a Foo Fighters song, "Hero," from the soundtrack as I rolled up. Of course, there was one last hitch . . . I forgot to fill it up with gas. We ended up pushing it to a gas station on the way and eventually made it to the opening. It was all worth it to see my best friend's face. ***Serves 1***

DRINK RATING

TRASHY   CLASSY

GLASSWARE

COUPE GLASS

SPECIAL TOOLS

Cocktail Shaker

✳

Muddler

SPIRITS

CHAMPAGNE COGNAC

GRAND MARNIER

---

3 lemon wedges

1 tablespoon brown sugar

2½ ounces Champagne cognac

1 ounce Grand Marnier

⅓ ounce egg whites

Garnish: Lemon or orange zest

In a cocktail shaker, muddle the lemon wedges with the brown sugar. Add the Champagne cognac, Grand Marnier, and egg whites. Shake without ice (this is called a dry shake). Add ice to shaker. Strain into a coupe glass. Garnish with lemon or orange zest.

Note

Like we said before, don't drink and drive. If you want a pic for the 'gram of you and a friend drinking a sidecar in a sidecar, just be sure it's safely parked in the driveway. Or make it a virgin before hitting the road.

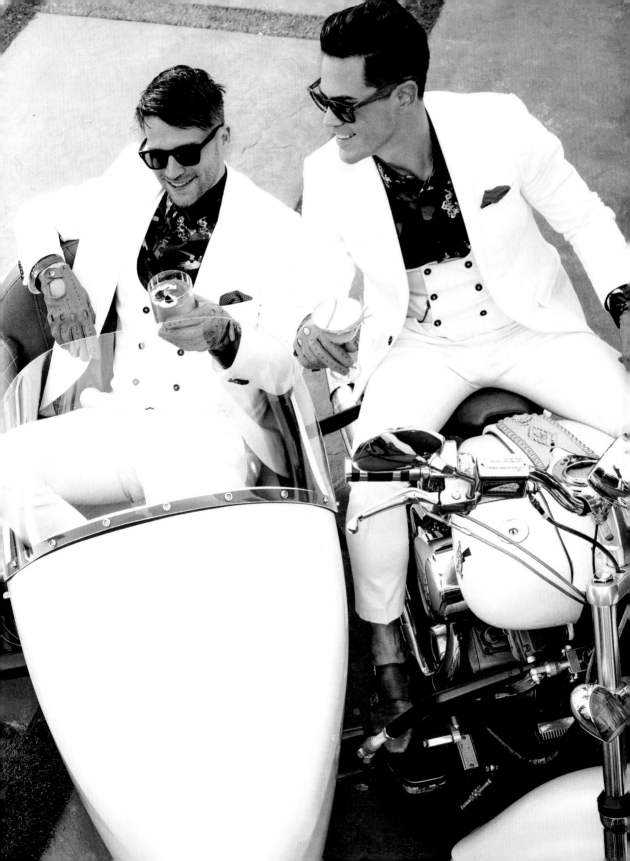

Stay-Cay

TOM ✳ In season 7 when the girls took their trip to Solvang, the guys decided to have their own stay-cation. You only saw some of it on TV. Peter had some fun in a bathroom, Jax and Beau decided to call their girlfriends, and I took out my bartending equipment and made some cocktails. We spent the next day at the pool, then went to get a clean shave and stopped at the Phoenix (a bar). By the time we got to the Phoenix, we were sleep-deprived and dehydrated. You saw Schwartz and me complaining about potentially not getting drinks on the menu at TomTom. If we hadn't gone so hard during our stay-cation, I don't think we would have been so intense about that on camera. Anyway, this drink recipe is something a little sweeter than I would normally drink, but it gives the essence of a vacation. *Serves 1*

1½ ounces citron vodka

¾ ounce Campari

½ ounce lemon juice

½ ounce orange juice

½ ounce light agave nectar

Champagne

Garnish: Lemon zest

In a cocktail shaker, mix the vodka, Campari, lemon juice, orange juice, and agave nectar. Fill the remainder of the shaker with ice. Shake and strain over fresh ice in a wine glass.

Garnish with lemon zest.

Note

You don't need a full kit to make a good drink, but a good bartending kit doesn't hurt. Most people find the cheapest one they can and then the cocktail shaker and tools end up breaking in the dishwasher or bending easily. If you can, spend a few extra dollars to buy a well-made bar kit. It will end up saving you money down the line because you won't have to buy a backup.

DRINK RATING

TRASHY   CLASSY

GLASSWARE

WINE GLASS

SPECIAL TOOL

Cocktail Shaker

SPIRITS

CITRON VODKA

CAMPARI

CHAMPAGNE

DRINK RATING

TRASHY   CLASSY

GLASSWARE

TALL GLASS

SPECIAL TOOLS

Muddler

SPIRIT

RUM

FRANKLIN ROSE
Mojïto

TOM ⟶ Ariana and I went to a charity auction for Vanderpump Dogs where we bid on, and won, a trip to Cuba. One of our guides in Cuba was named Franklin. Right when we met him, we told him we needed a mojito. Just as the words came out of our mouths, Franklin pulled out a laminated recipe card. "You gotta have a *real* mojito," he said. Franklin told us it was important to use aged rum, seven years or more. Crushed ice. Top with bitters. One of our stops was Santiago, where we noticed one of the bars was having a mojito-making competition. I entered and went last. They had cubed ice for the competitors that everyone used. When it came time for me to make the mojito, I wrapped the cubed ice in a napkin and banged it against the table to crush it. I won by a landslide, and the prize was aged rum. It was a full-circle moment. This recipe is an homage to Franklin. You don't have to use aged rum, but it will taste better if you do. *Serves 1*

¾ **ounce lime juice**

4 to 5 fresh mint sprigs

1 tablespoon rose-infused sugar

Crushed ice for serving

2 ounces aged rum

Garnish: 2 dashes bitters

In a tall glass, muddle the lime juice, mint, and sugar. Fill the remainder with crushed ice. Add the rum and stir.

Garnish with bitters.

Note

Franklin had this recipe ready to go, and it's good to have your favorite drink recipe handy. You might not want to carry around a recipe card, but you should know how to make your favorite drink. You never know when you'll be at a bar where the bartender is new or when you're at your friend's house and expected to mix your own. Don't be one of those people who only knows how to mix vodka and soda when you're at a house party.

Carrot Mule Variation

TOM ✴ This recipe is strange. (So am I, if we're being honest.) This idea came out of me thinking of the weirdest thing I could put in a Moscow mule to make it distinct. It took work to get it to taste just right, but once it was perfected, it became one of my favorite drinks. Also, mules like carrots, so it fits. *Serves 1*

2 ounces vodka

¾ ounce carrot juice

½ ounce lemon juice

Crushed or pebble ice for serving

½ cup ginger beer

Garnish: Baby carrots

In a copper mug, add the vodka, carrot juice, and lemon juice. Stir. Fill the remainder of the mug with crushed or pebble ice. Add the ginger beer.

Garnish with the baby carrots.

Note

For the garnish, baby carrots with green leaves look the best.

Feel the Lav

GLASSWARE

MARTINI GLASS

SPECIAL TOOLS

Cocktail Shaker

✷

Muddler

SPIRITS

VODKA

COINTREAU

ARIANA ⟶ I named this drink Feel the Lav because of the lavender, but it instantly reminded me of one of Tom's modeling sayings. He has all these tricks when he gets in front of the camera. My favorite is "Sun in the eyes, treasure in the distance." I think Tom learned it from Guillermo, but if you're trying to look sexy and serious, just imagine the sun is in your eyes and there is treasure in the distance, and you'll be fine. You can probably comb through this book and see Tom doing that exact face. You'll know exactly what I'm talking about when you see it. *Serves 1*

½ lemon

Sugar

½ ounce lavender syrup
(see below)

1½ ounces vodka

½ ounce Cointreau

Garnish: Lavender blossoms

Use a lemon wedge to dampen the rim of the glass. Dip the rim into sugar.

In a cocktail shaker, muddle the ½ lemon with the lavender syrup. Fill the remainder of the shaker with ice. Add the vodka and Cointreau. Shake and strain into the rimmed martini glass.

Garnish with lavender blossoms.

Note

Make sure you're garnishing with lavender blossoms. You don't want to pull a Solvang-Kristen and assume any old weed is lavender.

LAVENDER SYRUP

1 cup water ◆ 1 cup raw sugar ◆ 1 tablespoon dried lavender blossoms

Combine all ingredients in small saucepan. Bring to a boil. Stir until sugar dissolves. Simmer for 1 minute. Remove from the heat and let seep for 30 minutes. Strain out the lavender.

THE
Dumplin'

TOM → When Ariana and I first started dating, I had a very basic palate. I knew cocktails, but when it came to food, I was an infant. She opened my eyes to so many different things, including dumplings. She's so tiny that one day I called her my little dumplin', and the nickname stuck. We have other nicknames for each other. I call her my little boner, my poop stain. She calls me turd nugget. She's the big spoon. I'm the little spoon. She's also always so warm, I'll cuddle up in her arms when I'm cold. In those moments, I call her my little jacuzzi. I love her and some people may think our nicknames are cheesy, but as long as my dumplin' is happy, I'm happy. This drink is warm and cozy, just like Ariana. *Serves 1*

1½ ounces salted caramel liqueur

2 ounces bourbon

¾ ounce oat-infused caramel syrup (see below)

1 ounce oat milk

In a saucepan, combine the liqueur, bourbon, oat-infused caramel syrup, and oat milk. Stir. Once warm, pour into the mug. Serve hot.

Note

This drink goes best with a Nancy Meyers movie. Throw on your coziest sweater, cuddle up with a blanket, and watch Meryl/Cameron/Diane fall in love while you get drunk on your couch.

OAT-INFUSED CARAMEL SYRUP

1 cup water • 1 cup caramel syrup • ²/₃ cup (1 packet) cinnamon and spice-flavored instant oatmeal

Combine the water and syrup in a small saucepan. Bring to a boil. Add the oats. Reduce to a simmer, stirring until oatmeal softens, 2 to 4 minutes. Remove from the heat. Strain out the oats.

DRINK RATING

TRASHY   CLASSY

GLASSWARE

MUG

SPECIAL TOOLS

Saucepan

❋

Strainer

❋

Cozy Blanket

❋

Nancy Meyers Movie

SPIRITS

SALTED CARAMEL LIQUEUR

BOURBON

GLASSWARE

MUG

SPIRIT

BOURBON

Tom Toddy

TOM ⟶ This is a perfect winter drink. A few years back, Ariana and I went to Lake Tahoe for New Year's to snowboard. We got snowed in and we were forced to stay a couple extra days. We had plenty of time to try every possible hot toddy made in Lake Tahoe. We couldn't find one that we liked, so we decided to come up with our own. This one calls for almond milk because we don't drink too much dairy. This also incorporates chai, something Ariana turned me on to. On one of our first dates we went to a coffee shop. She ordered chai, and it was the first time I tried it. I loved it. This Tom Toddy recipe is great for those cold nights when you need a hot drink. It also has espresso, so it's also perfect for drinking before you hit the slopes. It will give you the kick of energy you need to tackle a day of winter sports. *Serves 1*

1 ounce unsweetened vanilla almond milk

6 ounces hot water

1 shot espresso

1 ounce bourbon

¾ ounce honey

Dash of cinnamon

1 chai tea bag

Garnish: Round lemon slice, cinnamon stick

In a mug, mix the almond milk, hot water, espresso, bourbon, honey, and cinnamon. Drop in a chai tea bag. Let sit for a couple of minutes.

Remove the tea bag and garnish with the lemon slice and cinnamon stick.

Serve hot.

Note

You can customize this cocktail by using your favorite tea.

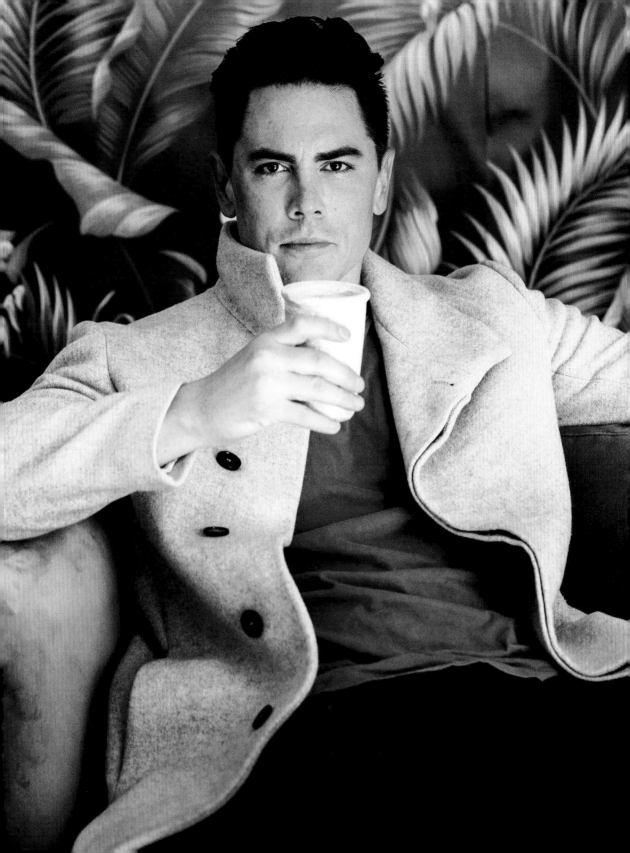

Bride-to-Be

ARIANA ✴ Weddings look beautiful on TV, but filming them can get a little tricky. On *Vanderpump Rules*, you've seen Schwartz and Katie get married, Scheana and Shay get married, and Jax and Brittany get married. Because of music rights, we either have to turn off the music or film in other locations for portions of the reception. This happens when we go on vacation, too. Producers will sometimes take over the DJ booths when we're at clubs with loud music. Occasionally they'll be able to work around the loud music, and other times the footage is shown in montages to avoid paying the licensing fees. Luckily we all know how to have a good time with or without a soundtrack. *Serves 1*

4 watermelon balls (see note)

⅓ ounce simple syrup (page 17)

⅓ ounce lemon juice

1 ounce watermelon vodka

½ ounce Chambord

Crushed ice for serving

Champagne

Garnish: Cinnamon

In a cocktail shaker, muddle the watermelon with the simple syrup. Add the lemon juice, vodka, and Chambord. Fill the remainder of the shaker with ice. Shake and strain over fresh crushed ice in a glass. Top with Champagne.

Garnish with a dash of cinnamon.

Note

We recommend four watermelon balls. If you don't have a melon baller, use a tablespoon. You'll muddle the balls anyway, so they just need to be roughly a half of a tablespoon in size. You can also substitute your favorite melon. If you're matching the colors of the wedding, use a melon that matches the décor.

DRINK RATING

TRASHY   CLASSY

GLASSWARE

WINE GLASS

SPECIAL TOOLS

Melon Baller

✴

Cocktail Shaker

✴

Muddler

SPIRITS

WATERMELON VODKA

CHAMBORD

CHAMPAGNE

TRASHY   CLASSY

GLASSWARE

ROCKS GLASS

SPECIAL TOOLS

Cocktail Shaker

✳

Eyedropper

SPIRIT

WHISKEY

LA Sour

ARIANA ✳ Everyone in LA is always doing a specialty diet. They're either gluten-free or sugar-free or following some fad. Not all the LA stereotypes are true, but this one is. CBD oil is helpful to many, but it can sometimes feel like it's another LA trend. That said, I love CBD oil and can't recommend it enough. *Serves 1*

2 ounces whiskey

¾ ounce lemon juice

½ ounce beet juice

¼ ounce honey

¼ ounce aquafaba (page 58)

15 mg CBD oil (2 to 3 drops, optional; see notes below and page 62)

In a cocktail shaker, mix the whiskey, lemon juice, beet juice, honey, and aquafaba. Using an eyedropper, add 2 to 3 drops of CBD oil. Fill the remainder of the shaker with ice. Shake and strain over fresh ice in a rocks glass.

Note

If you're looking for a high, and if you live in one of the states where cannabis is legal, look for a CBD oil with THC. Use with caution. Too much THC can cause a bad trip . . . we've heard.

THE ICONIC
Pellegrino

DANNY PELLEGRINO, COAUTHOR ＊ I've loved *Vanderpump Rules* since the beginning. There have been so many iconic and ridiculous moments—Kristen and Ariana fighting over comedy, the Jax and Frank Vegas fight, Stassi telling Scheana to get her a Pinot Grigio, the old lady who spent one of her final days asleep in the same bed that Jax and Faith hooked up in—I've loved it all. Like most viewers, I watch and judge the cast for their debauchery, often reducing them to messy, unlikeably likable reality TV characters. That changed in season 5. In the early hours of June 12, 2016, the Pulse nightclub shooting happened. Like many other gay men, I felt broken and lost watching the events unfold on the news. It was devastating. I live in West Hollywood, and the LA Gay Pride parade was the morning after the Pulse shooting. Many of us were scared to go to the parade. There were reports of another shooter on the loose in our area. Our community was trying to process an onslaught of emotions.

A few months later, *Vanderpump Rules* season 5, episode 6 aired. In the episode, we saw the group of SURvers we've been falling in love with waking up the morning of June 12, trying to decide if they should go into work during the parade. Understandably, the cast was visibly upset and very scared, just like my friends and I were that same morning. Seeing Tom Sandoval cry real tears over the devastating losses in Orlando touched me through the TV screen. He's cried many times on television, but this was the first time I saw one of my favorite reality TV stars crying similar tears and feeling similar fears. Ariana and Tom proudly went into SUR that day. They made drinks and entertained the LGBTQ+ community. Although it would be years until I met them in person and fell in love with their beautifully quirky personalities, I saw them as people through the TV screen that episode and I liked the people I saw. The Tom I've gotten to know is generous and unpredictable, sensitive and caring. Ariana is whip-smart and stunning, hilarious, and kind. On my podcast, *Everything Iconic*, I

CONTINUES

DRINK RATING

TRASHY   CLASSY

GLASSWARE

COLLINS GLASS

SPECIAL TOOLS

Cocktail Shaker

＊

Muddler

SPIRIT

LEMON VODKA

celebrate the absurdity of reality TV, which can often be a beautiful escape from our own realities. Every so often the real stuff sneaks in to our shows to remind us that we're all dealing with similar shit. For me that happened back in season 5 during that episode. For you, maybe it was watching Scheana go through a divorce at the same time you did. Or maybe you related to Katie when she opened up about her skylight accident. Or perhaps you haven't had that relatable moment and instead watch for the laughs. I'm grateful to *Vanderpump Rules* for giving me so many of those laughs throughout the years, and for the real and relatable moments that have snuck in. Tom and Ariana were kind enough to craft this drink on my behalf, and I couldn't have been more thrilled. Like all their cocktails, it's delicious. And if you're wondering what Tom and Ariana are like in person, I can honestly say they are iconic. *Serves 1*

2 lemon wedges

¼ ounce simple syrup (page 17)

2 ounces organic lemon vodka

Splash of pineapple juice

Sparkling water

Garnish: 2 to 3 thin slices of star fruit

In a cocktail shaker, muddle the lemon wedges with the simple syrup. Add the organic lemon vodka and a splash of pineapple juice. Fill the remainder of the shaker with ice. Shake and strain over fresh ice in a Collins glass. Top with sparkling water.

Garnish with star fruit.

Note

Most of the recipes in the book mix sweet and savory. This one is all sweet. If you prefer less sweetness, shake the ingredients with ice a few more times before straining into the glass. That will cause the ice to dilute the ingredients a touch more before serving. For the garnish, we used honey to adhere the star fruit to the sides of the glass before straining the liquid in. You don't have to do this; it just enhances the presentation.

THE
DILF

ARIANA ✳ We call this The DILF because it has a dill in it and we thought the name was cute, but we know you're all thinking it stands for "Dads I'd Like to F*ck." None of the men on our show have kids . . . yet. You *have* seen dads on our show, though. There is the obvious DILF, Guillermo. We know you all think he's sexy. Ken is around too, but who can compete with the Argentinian George Clooney?

Aside from those two, our relationships with our fathers are shown from time to time. My dad passed away around season 3, but Tom's dad has popped up a few times. I'm not saying he's a DILF, but he's a *very* handsome and wonderful man. Aside from being great at karaoke (he can do everything from Sinatra to "Every Rose Has Its Thorn"), he's a true survivor. A few seasons ago, Tom filmed a scene with his dad, Tony, and my brother Jeremy. Despite being very healthy, Tony had a freak heart attack that left him in the ICU. In the conversation they talked about what happened to Tony. Tears were shed, and everyone in the room was reminded how life is so fleeting. The three of them didn't expect to have such an emotional talk that day, but sometimes life lessons sneak in when you least expect them. Tony is alive today and Tom hugs him a little tighter knowing he was so close to losing him. They never aired the moment of them talking about life. Maybe it would've been a little too heavy. Hell, maybe it's a little too heavy to include in a book of cocktails, but that's life isn't it? Hold your loved ones tight and let the DILFs in your life know they're appreciated. *Serves 1*

3 cucumber slices

1 sprig fresh dill

¼ ounce agave nectar

1½ ounces Hendrick's gin

1¼ ounces lemon juice

1 ounce St. Germain elderflower liqueur

Club soda

Garnish: Cucumber slice, dill sprig

In a cocktail shaker, muddle the cucumber, fresh dill, and agave nectar. Add the Hendrick's, lemon juice, and St. Germain. Fill the remainder of the shaker with ice. Shake and strain into a short glass. Top with splash of club soda.

Garnish with a cucumber slice and a dill sprig.

DRINK RATING

TRASHY   CLASSY

GLASSWARE

SHORT GLASS

SPECIAL TOOLS

Muddler

✳

Cocktail Shaker

SPIRITS

HENDRICK'S GIN

ST. GERMAIN ELDERFLOWER LIQUEUR

THE DILF, PAGE 87

GLASSWARE

TALL GLASS

SPIRITS

GOLDSCHLÄGER
AMARETTO LIQUEUR

LUXURY
High-Rise

TOM ⟶ This was the first cocktail I ever created. I've always been a creative person, and I was able to channel my creativity into making drinks. When I first started, I noticed everyone was ordering cocktails with energy drinks mixed in. The Hollywood bars are filled with people who want to stay up as late as possible and there are only a few ways to do that. I couldn't serve drinks with cocaine in them, so I created something a little classier. It might not give you wings, but it will keep you awake until the 2:00 a.m. last call. *Serves 1*

2 ounces Goldschläger

¾ ounce amaretto liqueur

¾ ounce orange energy drink

Garnish: Orange slice

In a tall glass, mix the Goldschläger, amaretto liqueur, and energy drink. Fill with ice. Stir. Garnish with an orange slice.

Note

An orange-flavored energy drink works best, but you can substitute your favorite flavor or even use a sugar-free option.

Self-Indulgent

ARIANA ✳ Tom has a sweet tooth. He loves cookies in particular. Every year around Christmas, his mom will make ten different cookies and send them our way. It's the one time a year where he'll buy regular milk, and I'll see him dipping the cookies into it. Problem is, he has no self-control with them. He'll gorge and then feel sick. He's definitely a cookie monster. This drink is for people with a sweet tooth. We have our healthy-ish version of a mudslide, and this is the opposite of that. It's a dessert in a glass. *Serves 1*

½ ounce Goldschläger

½ ounce coffee liqueur

½ ounce Frangelico

½ ounce Baileys Irish Cream

½ ounce white chocolate liqueur

½ ounce dark chocolate liqueur

Garnish: White and dark chocolate shavings (see note)

In a cocktail shaker, put the Goldschläger, coffee-flavored liqueur, Frangelico, Baileys, white chocolate liqueur, and dark chocolate liqueur. Fill the remainder of the shaker with ice. Shake and strain into a martini glass.

Top with white and dark chocolate shavings.

Note

You can use a vegetable peeler to make chocolate shavings. You can also use a knife to shave thin shavings from a large piece of chocolate. This is a dessert drink, so the more chocolate, the better.

GLASSWARE

MARTINI GLASS

SPECIAL TOOLS

Cocktail Shaker

✳

Vegetable Peeler

SPIRITS

GOLDSCHLÄGER

COFFEE LIQUEUR

FRANGELICO

BAILEYS IRISH CREAM

WHITE CHOCOLATE LIQUEUR

DARK CHOCOLATE LIQUEUR

ARIANA ✳ Tom and I both lived in New York before moving to California. I went to Flagler College in Florida, spent my summers at NYU, and moved to NYC for a few memorable years before making the move to LA. I love the city so much. During those NYU summers, I made some lifelong friends and had some crazy roommates, including a party girl who propositioned me for a threesome with a guy she was sleeping with. I politely declined, but years later I found myself being pulled into the backseat of a car in a similar scenario.

The show brings us back to New York quite a bit. During the season, we visit *Watch What Happens Live* often. Sometimes the cast is paired with a random celebrity, but Scheana often finds herself paired with cable news personas. She's been paired with Wolf Blitzer and S.E. Cupp and has been known to watch the news all day to catch up before the show. WWHL is always fun, but much like the time I get to spend in NYC with my friends, it moves so quickly. We answer a few questions, play a game, film an aftershow for BravoTV.com, take a few pictures, and it's over! Andy is always a blast to be around!

New Yorkers are thought to be a little salty, but I always thought of that as a good thing. It takes a thick skin to thrive in NYC. *Serves 1*

2 ounces bourbon

1 ounce caramel liqueur

½ ounce sweet vermouth

Dash of orgeat syrup

½ ounce aquafaba (page 58)

2 drops bitters

Garnish: Salted caramel chew, attitude

In a cocktail shaker, mix the bourbon, liqueur, vermouth, and orgeat syrup. Fill the remainder of the shaker with ice. Shake and strain into a coupe glass. Top with the aquafaba. Use an eyedropper to put 2 drops of bitters on top of the aquafaba. Drag a toothpick through them to make a spiral.

Garnish with a salted caramel chew and a lot of attitude.

Note

If you don't like spicy,
forgo the garnish.

Gentlemen's Curse

TOM → This drink is dedicated to Vintage Jax because he was his own biggest curse. The two of us met years ago in Miami when we were struggling models. All the New York models would fly to Miami for the winter to pre-shoot summer campaigns. Neither of us had any money, so we would stay wherever we could. There was one point where Jax and I even shared a twin bed. Years later, after Schwartz became my roommate in LA, Jax was desperate. He needed a place to stay. I let him crash on my couch, but he quickly partitioned off the living room with a bedsheet. Overnight, my apartment became a frat house with the three of us. Vintage Jax would bring home and hook up with random girls. There was only a bedsheet separating us from them. We would hear a plethora of things told to these girls. "You're different than all the other girls here." "You're the kind of girl I would settle down and have kids with." "It's crazy I'm meeting someone like you in LA. Girls here are so fake." "It's fate I'm meeting you." It was all bullshit.

I call this drink the Gentlemen's Curse because Vintage Jax would say gentleman-like things to these girls, but would be cursed by the words he could never live up to. Jax's flings didn't last, but the friendship of Schwartz, Jax, and me did. We reminisce, laugh at those times, and even give each other shit for them. We think about the things we did to get by, which included a lot of going out and crazy adventures. These guys are like family. Jax is much more secure in himself now, so the need to try to be someone else has become obsolete. I think his relationship with Brittany has broken the curse. *Serves 1*

1 ounce mezcal

½ ounce Amaro Averna

½ ounce ginger liqueur

½ ounce St. Germain elderflower liqueur

¾ ounce lime juice

¼ ounce egg whites

Garnish: Chili powder

In a cocktail shaker, add the mezcal, Amaro Averna, ginger liqueur, St. Germain, lime juice, and egg whites. Fill the remainder of the shaker with ice. Shake and strain into a coupe glass.

Garnish with chili powder.

DRINK RATING

TRASHY   CLASSY

GLASSWARE

COUPE GLASS

SPECIAL TOOL

Cocktail Shaker

SPIRITS

MEZCAL

AMARO AVERNA

GINGER LIQUEUR

ST. GERMAIN ELDERFLOWER LIQUEUR

TNT

TRASHY   CLASSY

GLASSWARE

SHORT GLASS

SPECIAL TOOLS

Cocktail Shaker

✹

Muddler

SPIRIT

HABANERO TEQUILA

ARIANA ⊹ I call this the TNT because it feels like a bomb in your mouth. There have been many metaphorical bombs thrown around throughout the seasons of *Vanderpump Rules*. In season 6, there was an explosion after the reveal of an infamous recording. That night is remembered for what happened between Jax and Brittany, but it was one of the biggest fights I've had with Tom. Tom thought it was bad timing to reveal this bombshell of a recording to Brittany. In an ideal world, yes, we would have sat her down at a quiet, secluded lunch, but it's not an ideal world. We were drunk. It happened. I think I even threw an empty plastic cup at Tom at one point. Once I was home, I realized I left my phone at Brittany's! Around 3:30 a.m., I walked back. I heard the Dixie Chicks and the *Moana* soundtrack blaring from Brittany's apartment. Katie and Kristen were singing it out with Brittany, while Jax was hiding over at Schwartz's apartment with Tom. I got to sing out my frustrations with my girls and I found my phone. Sometimes people think our nights end when the camera crew goes home, but when we need a girls' sing-along in the middle of the night, we are always there for each other. *Serves 1*

3 lime wedges

Jalapeño salt

¼ ounce light agave nectar

1½ ounces habanero tequila

1 ounce blood orange juice (see note)

Garnish: Blood orange slice

Dampen the rim of the glass with a lime wedge. Dip the rim into jalapeño salt.

In a cocktail shaker, muddle all the lime wedges with the agave nectar. Add the tequila and blood orange juice. Fill the remainder of the shaker with ice. Shake and strain into a glass over fresh ice.

Garnish with the blood orange slice.

Note

Blood orange juice tastes a bit different than regular OJ. You can easily sub regular juice, but the blood orange is tart, so just know you will be missing that flavor.

PART TWO

Trashy

GLASSWARE

SHORT
GLASS

SPECIAL TOOLS

Cocktail Shaker
Lighter
Fire Extinguisher
Magician's Cape

SPIRITS

GIN

GREEN
CHARTREUSE

FAILED MAGICIAN

<u>**TOM**</u> Sometimes bartenders like to do tricks to get extra bucks. Ever have someone serve you a drink that was on fire? Customers are usually impressed when there is a flame coming off their cocktail. The bartender either wanted to impress you with their skills or get a few extra dollars. I call this the Failed Magician because to a magician, a little fire is nothing, but to a bartender, fire is everything. You may not get hired at the Magic Castle for this little fire trick, but you can get a gig slinging drinks at your local bar and restaurant. **SERVES 1**

1½ ounces gin
3 tablespoons mango sorbet
¾ ounce fresh lemon juice
Dash of habanero shrub
Crushed ice for serving

GARNISH: *Halved and hollowed out small lemon, ½ ounce Green Chartreuse*

Add the gin, mango sorbet, lemon juice, and dash of shrub to a cocktail shaker. Fill the remainder of the shaker with ice. Shake and strain into a short glass over fresh crushed ice.

For garnish, fill the half lemon with the Chartreuse. Carefully light on fire and serve with the cocktail. Blow out the flame and pour the Chartreuse into the drink.

note *Don't play with fire unless you're confident in your skills. Even then, be sure to have a fire extinguisher handy! In fact, even if you aren't making this drink, be sure to have a fire extinguisher in your house.*

CRYMAX

TOM The Crymax is a *Vanderpump* cast special. Before the show even started, we would drink this on the job. Everyone assumed we were sipping soda water mixed with juice. It was our way of sneaking alcohol when we had a free moment. You would see these drinks everywhere—in the employee bathroom, the kitchen, the supply closet. Schwartz named it the Crymax because his drink was often the catalyst for a phenomenal cry, a beautiful climax, or a mix of both. Hence the name, Crymax. If you want to concoct this like us, just throw some white wine, club soda, and a few muddled strawberries in some crushed ice and stir. We didn't have time to get fancy when there was a line of people waiting to order drinks.

Those early SUR days were fun. We had no idea if people would watch the show. We were struggling SURvers trying to SURvive Los Angeles. If we're being honest with ourselves, we're all still trying to SURvive Los Angeles, but at least we aren't sneaking a Crymax during our shifts. **SERVES 1**

5 ounces Pinot Grigio

½ ounce Grand Marnier

1½ ounces strawberry puree (see below)

2 ounces soda water

1 lemon wedge

Add ice to a tall glass. Add the Pinot Grigio, Grand Marnier, and strawberry puree. Stir lightly to mix. Top with the soda water. Squeeze the juice from the lemon wedge on top, drop in a straw, and enjoy!

note

On Vanderpump Rules, *the cast is often seen in the back alley. That SUR dumpster has seen a lot of tears. When a friend is crying, it's great to mix them a fancier drink that will lull them out of their sadness. This is that drink. Perfect for crying by the dumpster, or a fancy cocktail hour.*

STRAWBERRY PUREE

5 strawberries

2 ounces water

2 ounces Splenda

To make the strawberry puree, remove the green tops from 5 strawberries. Slice the strawberries and combine in a blender with 2 ounces water and 2 ounces Splenda or regular sugar. Blend until smooth and chill until needed.

DRINK RATING

TRASHY   CLASSY

GLASSWARE

TALL
GLASS

SPECIAL TOOLS

Reusable Straw

SPIRITS

PINOT GRIGIO

GRAND MARNIER

GLASSWARE

TALL
GLASS

SPECIAL TOOL

Saucepan

SPIRITS

DATE WHISKEY

HONEY LIQUEUR

RUMCHATA

CEREAL DATER

<u>ARIANA</u> A serial dater is someone who thinks they need a boyfriend or girlfriend. They fall in love right away and break up shortly after. The full cycle of the relationship is quick, and then they move on to the next person. They are constantly in one of these relationships that ultimately go nowhere. This cocktail is inspired by those relationships. If you're in one, make this breakfast cocktail and relish the temporary bliss of your temporary love. **SERVES 1**

1 ounce date whiskey (see below)

¾ ounce honey liqueur

1½ ounces RumChata

2 dashes almond bitters

GARNISH: *Pitted date, Honey Bunches of Oats cereal*

In tall glass over ice, add the whiskey, liqueur, Rumchata, and almond bitters. Stir.

For garnish, cut a pitted date in half and roll in Honey Bunches of Oats cereal. Stick on the side of the glass.

 This is a morning drink. The taste of cereal has such a nostalgic effect. It reminds me of being a kid. You can drink it any time, but it's great for brunch if you want something sweet and strong that will take you back in time.

DATE WHISKEY

1 750-ml bottle 100-proof rye whiskey

15 to 20 chopped dates

Heat the whiskey and dates in saucepan over low heat, covered, for 5 minutes. Let sit for 1½ hours. Filter out the dates with a strainer.

NOTE: You can also use a sous vide bath to heat your date whiskey. The process is slower, but the flavors will blend well. Or if you have even more time, put the chopped dates into a bottle of whiskey and let sit for 5 to 7 days before straining.

Cereal Dater PAGE 106

MAD MADIX

ARIANA I don't get drunk that often, especially on TV. However, I do loosen up a bit more when we take our cast trips. That time in season 7 when you saw me rambling about Yellow Robe Smith, I think I was trying to say that everyone goes through shit, and we're all heroes of our own stories. I wanted to say that you can't compare your pain to another person's pain. Unfortunately, that's not what came out. Sometimes the alcohol does the talking for you. The next morning was rough, but Stassi gave me a hangover patch that lessened my pain. **SERVES 1**

2 mandarin orange wedges

Tajin seasoning

1 sprig fresh cilantro

¼ ounce scorpion chile-infused honey (Bee Local Hot Honey, made in Portland by Jacobsen Salt Co.)

1½ ounces spicy tequila

Sparkling Orange Celsius

Dash of tabasco sauce

GARNISH: *Tabasco, sprig of cilantro (optional)*

Dampen the rim of the glass with an orange wedge. Dip the rim into the Tajin seasoning.

In a cocktail shaker, muddle the orange wedges and sprig of cilantro with the honey. Fill the remainder of the shaker with ice. Add the tequila. Shake and strain into a serving glass over fresh ice. Top with Celsius.

Garnish with a dash of Tabasco and sprig of cilantro, if desired.

note *When you're rimming a glass, you can moisten with any juice you have. You just need something sticky enough to hold the salt or seasoning. Drink until you're making snow angels on the floor of your Mexican hotel.*

GLASSWARE

TALL
GLASS

SPECIAL TOOL

Cocktail Shaker

Muddler

SPIRIT

SPICY TEQUILA

GLASSWARE

MASON
JAR

SPECIAL TOOLS

Cocktail Shaker

Muddler

Lo-Fi Filter

SPIRIT

VODKA

CITRON CLEANSE

ARIANA People in LA hike. A lot. And then they want something reasonably healthy to quench their thirst. And everyone is always doing a fucking cleanse. You can be out on a Friday night with a friend who is blacked out and they will still make plans to work out the next morning. It may sound backwards, but people are doing their best. This cocktail is that mix of health and gluttony. Low-cal, but still boozy. And remember, you're doing great, sweetie. **SERVES 1**

2 lemon wedges

4 drops liquid stevia

3 cucumber slices

¼ ounce liquid charcoal (optional)

Pinch of cayenne pepper (optional)

2 ounces organic artisanal vodka

½ ounce grapefruit juice

Sparkling water

GARNISH: *Kale leaf*

In a cocktail shaker, muddle the lemon, stevia, and cucumber slices. If desired, add the liquid charcoal and pinch of cayenne pepper to aid in a speedier metabolism and detoxification. Fill the remainder of the shaker with ice. Add the vodka and juice. Shake well and pour into a mason jar over fresh ice, or into a BPA-free tumbler you can hike with. Top with sparkling water.

Garnish with kale.

Go on a hike and take a bunch of selfies so we know you went. Not necessary to hike all the way to the top. Selfie while you drink. Post on Instagram using a filter. #Cleanse #FitFam #FancyAF

PREGAME

TOM I love being a MacGyver when it comes to cocktails. These drinks are the most surprising because you would think that if they are made with a water bottle and basic condiments, they must taste like shit. These are incredibly cheap to make, but that doesn't mean they will taste cheap. I would imagine most of this stuff is lying around your apartment now. Give it a go and I bet you'll be surprised. **SERVES 1**

2 ounces whiskey

2 McDonald's BBQ sauce packets

1 packet honey

1 packet sugar

Water

If you only have a water bottle to mix this in, add the whiskey to the second line in the bottle and the BBQ sauce to third line. Each line denotes an ounce. Add the honey and sugar to the bottle. Fill the bottle with water until all ingredients reach the middle line. Put the cap back on. Shake vigorously. Pour over fresh ice.

DRINK RATING

TRASHY   CLASSY

GLASSWARE

anything

SPECIAL TOOL

Empty Water Bottle

SPIRIT

WHISKEY

TRASHY   CLASSY

GLASSWARE

anything

SPECIAL TOOL

Empty Water Bottle

SPIRIT

VODKA

BLOODY DESPERATE

ARIANA I love a bloody mary. It's a perfect hair-of-the-dog breakfast cocktail when you're hung over from a late night of Alanis Morrissette karaoke ("You Oughta Know" is my go-to). We created a Bloody Desperate Mary that is great for brunch, but it also works when you want an elevated dorm-room libation. Those of you in college will appreciate the craftiness of this recipe because you probably have all this stuff lying around your dorm or sorority house. The rest of you may be rolling your eyes at the idea of making a drink with leftover ketchup packets and an empty water bottle, but I promise the only rolling your eyes will do is rolling into the back of your head from the pure bliss of drinking one of these. Plus, you can screw the cap back on your water bottle and carry it to brunch with you. No one will look twice. #BYOBtoB **SERVES 1**

2 ounces vodka

1 ounce water

3 fast-food ketchup packets

2 Cholula hot sauce packets

Splash of pickle juice (optional)

GARNISH: *Pepper packet*

If you only have a water bottle to mix this in, add the vodka to the second line in the bottle and add the water to the third line. Each line denotes an ounce. Add the ketchup, hot sauce, and pickle juice if desired. Put the cap back on the bottle and shake. Pour over ice to serve.

Garnish with pinch of pepper from the pepper packet.

I have more than a few friends whose cars are loaded with empty water bottles. If you're one of those people, what are you waiting for? Save one for the Bloody Desperate and recycle the rest.

THE SURVIVALIST

TOM A lot of people who watch *Vanderpump Rules* think we have some sort of deal with Taco Bell. We are constantly eating it on the show. There's even a Taco Bell–inspired dish on the menu at TomTom. There's no crazy deal, we just fucking love it. The Survivalist is another one of those mix-in-an-empty-water-bottle beverages. This one calls for maple syrup and FIRE Sauce. I always have those T-Bell sauces in my car from late-night drive-thru runs, and I may have mixed this once or twice at a pancake house in the middle of the night using their table syrup. This recipe couldn't be trashier. F*ck it, when times become dire you gotta be a SURvivor. **SERVES 1**

2 ounces tequila

2 ounces water

1½ ounces maple syrup

1 packet Taco Bell FIRE Sauce

3 drops hot sauce such as Tabasco

If you only have a water bottle to mix this in, add tequila to the second line in the bottle and water to the fourth line. Each line denotes an ounce. Add the maple syrup and FIRE Sauce. Mix in 3 drops of hot sauce for extra spice. Put the cap back on the bottle. Shake. Pour over ice in whatever glass you can find.

note

These trashy drinks can all be elevated using professional bartending equipment and high-quality ingredients. For this one, I recommend using the finest tequila you can find and organic aged maple syrup from Vermont, but don't try to replace the Taco Bell sauce. It's one-of-a-kind.

DRINK RATING

TRASHY   CLASSY

GLASSWARE

anything

SPECIAL TOOL

Empty Water Bottle

SPIRIT

TEQUILA

DRINK RATING

TRASHY   CLASSY

GLASSWARE

FLASK

SPECIAL TOOLS

Saucepan

Stealth

SPIRIT

WHATEVER YOU HAVE

TRESPASSER

<u>**TOM**</u> This is for those outdoor concerts where you're not supposed to bring outside food or drink, but you don't have the money to buy the $20 cocktails they're selling. Just ask for a cup with ice when you get inside, and pour some of this into your cup. Or better yet, just take shots straight from the flask. **SERVES 1**

Booze
1 can favorite soft drink

note

You can add more soda reduction depending on your tastes. Add to the desired sweetness.

Heat up a soft drink of your choice in a saucepan over medium-high heat until it starts to boil. Reduce heat to low and let simmer until soft drink has reduced to roughly a sixth of the original amount, about 30 minutes. Turn off the heat and allow to cool. Pour 1 tablespoon of the soda reduction into a flask. Fill the remainder of the flask with alcohol of your choice. Close the flask and shake to mix. Sneak it into a concert. Pour over a cup of ice at the event.

TEQUILA KATIE

ARIANA Tequila Katie is a very prominent character on *Vanderpump Rules*. She may not always be around—she shows up late-night after Katie Maloney has left the building—but when she does make an appearance, it's noteworthy. We all have our alter egos when we booze. If you don't, I highly recommend creating one. People just call me Drunk Ariana when I'm drinking. Alcohol affects some of us more than others, and for Katie it brings out a unique side to her. Tequila Katie is bound to rage-text (see below), yell, and make a scene regardless of where she is. We named a cocktail after her because everyone needs to bring out their beautiful, inner Tequila Katie every once in a while. **SERVES 1**

Lime wedge

Chili salt

2 ounces tequila

½ ounce cucumber juice

¾ ounce fresh lime juice

½ ounce agave nectar

½ ounce beet juice

Crushed ice for serving

GARNISH: *Cucumber ribbon*

Use lime wedge to dampen the rim of the glass. Coat the rim with chili salt and set aside.

In a cocktail shaker, combine the tequila, cucumber juice, lime juice, agave nectar, and beet juice. Fill the remainder of the shaker with ice. Shake well and strain over fresh crushed ice in the rimmed glass.

Garnish with a cucumber ribbon.

8:43

TS XM

2 People >

Jul 21, 2016, 8:23 PM

Katie Maloney

I'm tired of fighting and defending myself against y'all with my fiancé. Jesus Christ. Get our yourselves.

And considering I already have the rep of texting "mean shit" I don't care.

We fight solely about him defending the two of you. Im very over it.

Y'all are very much his friends and it's hard to argue that. But I'm Very upset and frustrated.

note

Be careful with this one because of the beet juice. It'll stain worse than the blood of Katie's fallen enemies.

DRINK RATING

TRASHY   CLASSY

GLASSWARE

SHORT
GLASS

SPECIAL TOOL

Cocktail Shaker

SPIRIT

TEQUILA

DRINK RATING

TRASHY   CLASSY

GLASSWARE

ROCKS
GLASS

SPIRIT

BLANCO TEQUILA

I DON'T DO COKE

TOM If you are like me, someone who doesn't like to put anything up your nose, but you want to be able to hang with your friends and last, this is the drink for you. Maybe you need that extra boost. This recipe is for the people trying to keep their eyes open to watch the sunrise with the rest of the group. It will give you the energy of "pasta," but won't upset your stomach or give you the jitters like coffee or energy drinks. **SERVES 1**

1½ ounces blanco tequila

½ scoop Light Up Organic Energy Drink powder

2 squeezes of lime

Lemon-lime soda

In a rocks glass, mix the tequila and energy powder until the powder dissolves. Add ice. Squeeze in the lime juice and top with lemon-lime soda.

note *You can substitute your favorite energy drink for the powder. This drink is designed to keep you up at night, so drink with caution.*

STONER ROOMMATE

TOM We've already established that I have a sweet tooth. When I get stoned, I want candy. You may be shaking your head if you're looking at this recipe sober, but I promise if you get high and try it, you'll be in love. **SERVES 1**

10 to 15 sour gummies

1 ounce water

2 ounces vodka

1½ ounces lemon-lime soda

In a microwave-safe bowl, microwave sour gummies with water for 1 minute. Stir and heat another 30 seconds. Stir and repeat as needed until it makes a syrup that you can easily use as a mixer. In a short glass, pour the vodka and soda over ice. Add the melted gummies. Stir.

note

This drink is for stoners. Replace the sour gummies with whatever gummy candy you like. Drink alongside pizza/tacos/ice cream/ pasta. Choose one color gummy if you want the cocktail to look a certain way.

DRINK RATING

TRASHY   CLASSY

GLASSWARE

SHORT
GLASS

SPECIAL TOOLS

Microwave Bowl

SPIRIT

VODKA

GLASSWARE

COUPE
GLASS

SPECIAL TOOL

Cocktail Shaker

SPIRITS

JÄGERMEISTER

TEQUILA

CHAMPAGNE

SHITTY ROOMMATE

TOM I've had so many shitty roommates. Fortunately, I live with Ariana now, but throughout all my years in Los Angeles I've had some awful people living under the same roof as me. This drink is perfect for those assholes that you hate. It will cause them to have a horrendous hangover. They will drink it up and not know just how bad it is until morning. Just be sure to only serve this if your roommate has their own bathroom, because it will cause them to hug the toilet. We added liquid laxative as the icing on top to pay back the shitty roommate. In reality, it might be best to leave out the laxative. We're not trying to poison anyone. **SERVES 1**

½ ounce Jägermeister

½ ounce tequila

½ ounce bad margarita mix

½ ounce Champagne

Liquid laxative (just kidding, do NOT add this)

In a cocktail shaker, mix the Jägermeister, tequila, margarita mix, and Champagne. Fill the remainder of the shaker with ice. Shake and strain into the most beautiful coupe glass you can find.

Hand to your roommate and tell them it's called "The Bestie." Watch in glee as they drink a horrible drink.

note

This drink works best with the absolute worst ingredients because you're really just fucking with your terrible roommate, so be sure to buy the cheapest Champagne, a margarita mix filled with as many preservatives as possible, and maybe an extra-strength liquid laxative to top (again, just kidding!).

TOMTOM

TOM Opening TomTom was a dream come true. To be doing it with one of my best friends made it even more special. Schwartz and I are so proud of how beautiful the bar ended up. The design is flawless, the food is fantastic, and the cocktails are phenomenal. *LA Travel Magazine* voted the bar "best bar" in 2019, and we've seen so many celebrities walk through those doors. Kelly Clarkson, Pharrell, Chrissy Teigen, John Legend, Lady Gaga, and Selena Gomez have all stopped by, and on any given night you're likely to see someone from *Vanderpump Rules* relaxing with one of the specialty drinks. Schwartz loves the taste of Jäger, so this is for him. **SERVES 1**

4 fresh mint leaves

½ ounce Taylor's Velvet Falernum liqueur

¾ ounce lime juice

1½ ounces pineapple rum

½ ounce Jägermeister

Mint lemonade kombucha

In a cocktail shaker, muddle the mint leaves, falernum, and lime juice. Fill the remainder of the shaker with ice. Add the rum and Jägermeister. Shake and strain into a Collins glass over fresh ice. Top with kombucha.

note

Kombucha comes in many different flavors, and you can also make your own at home. We tend to use mint lemonade kombucha in our cocktails, but you can go with whatever you prefer.

DRINK RATING

TRASHY   CLASSY

GLASSWARE

COLLINS
GLASS

SPECIAL TOOLS

Cocktail Shaker

Muddler

SPIRITS

VELVET FALERNUM LIQUEUR

PINEAPPLE RUM

JÄGERMEISTER

LONG ISLAND

ARIANA If someone orders a Long Island, I know they aren't going to leave a great tip. That's because, typically, they want to get as fucked up as possible for the cheapest amount. They know Long Islands are full of various liquors and will make them very sloppy, very fast. The customer thinks they'll be able to pay for just one drink and get drunk for the night. They don't realize that Long Islands cost more than other cocktails because they have so many different types of liquor. When you ring up the drink, they hear the price and instantly take it out on the bartender. That means little or no tip. Not only that, customers will often want to *taste* the alcohol. Most people don't want to taste the alcohol in other mixed drinks, but that's not the case for Long Islands. People want to know that they are getting their money's worth with a Long Island, so they know they are getting drunk. I set out to make a Long Island that tasted good and will still get you drunker than me on the season 7 Mexico trip. #YellowRobeSmith. **SERVES 1**

GLASSWARE

TALL
GLASS

SPECIAL TOOLS

Cocktail Shaker

Muddler

SPIRITS

TEQUILA

VODKA

GIN

TRIPLE SEC

3 lemon wedges

¼ ounce simple syrup (page 17)

¾ ounce tequila

¾ ounce vodka

¾ ounce gin

¾ ounce triple sec

Cola (see note)

GARNISH: *Lemon wedge*

In a cocktail shaker, muddle the lemon wedges with the simple syrup. Add the tequila, vodka, gin, and triple sec. Fill the remainder of the shaker with ice. Shake and pour into a tall glass over fresh ice. Top with cola.

Garnish with a lemon wedge.

note

Make this drink lighter by using diet cola.

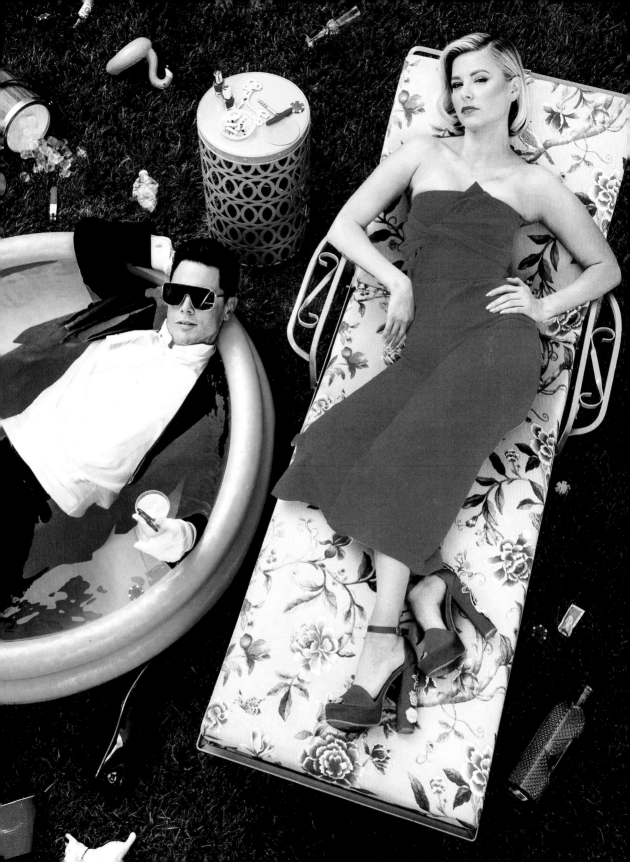

BASIC BITCH

ARIANA This drink is an ode to basics. Stassi refers to herself as "basic" and even wrote a book called *Next Level Basic*. When I met Stassi, I thought she was annoying. I thought she was playing a character. She was a little princess who, to me, seemed to have only-child syndrome (even though she isn't an only child). She pretended to be in charge of everyone around her. You can see that in the early seasons of the show. She wasn't for me. She was basic. That is, until I really got to know her and realized we have more in common than I thought. Once we put our differences aside, we became friends. I needed to embrace the basicness in the same way that she did. This drink is perfect for basics because of one very important feature: it photographs well for Instagram. Just be careful, because a few of these might bring out your inner Dark Passenger. **SERVES 1**

2 ounces vodka

¾ ounce Cointreau

½ ounce pomegranate liqueur

¾ ounce pineapple juice

GARNISH: *Lemon wedge*

In a cocktail shaker, add the vodka, Cointreau, pomegranate liqueur, and pineapple juice. Fill the remainder of the shaker with ice. Shake and strain into a martini glass. Garnish with a lemon wedge. Light your favorite scented candle to enjoy while drinking.

note

Live, laugh, love.

GLASSWARE

MARTINI
GLASS

SPECIAL TOOLS

Cocktail Shaker

Three-Wick Scented Candle

SPIRITS

VODKA

COINTREAU

POMEGRANATE LIQUEUR

GLASSWARE

TALL
GLASS

SPECIAL TOOLS

Muddler
Pump Sessions CD

SPIRITS

ST. GERMAIN
ELDERFLOWER
LIQUEUR

VODKA

DJ LIGHTWEIGHT

TOM James isn't a great drinker. You've seen it on the show. He has one too many and says things he *should* regret. A lot of time, he gets into trouble because he is such a lightweight. I've known people who could drink a bottle of vodka and still walk a straight line, and other people who can consume half a glass of wine and slur every other word out of their mouth. James is closer to the latter. **SERVES 1**

3 raspberries

1 ounce St. Germain elderflower liqueur

Splash of vodka

2 ounces sugar-free energy drink

Soda water

Muddle the raspberries in a tall glass. Fill the remainder of the glass with ice. Add the St. Germain, vodka, and sugar-free energy drink. Stir. Top with soda water.

note This is designed for lightweights. Add more vodka (2 ounces total) if you're serving to someone who can hold their liquor.

SUGAR BABY

ARIANA Everyone thinks Lala is a hardass. She is tough, but she's also soft and sweet. People can often see us as archetypes. You have the villains, the dumb ones, the girl-next-doors, and the lovable rascals (Schwartz). What you see on *Vanderpump Rules* of us *is* us, but we are more than what you see once a week. This cocktail is dedicated to the Lala you see onscreen. Suck it down, find a sugar daddy, and maybe you'll get a free Range Rover. **SERVES 1**

3 lime wedges

½ ounce simple syrup (page 17)

1 ounce strawberry puree (page 105)

2 ounces peach vodka

Champagne

In a cocktail shaker, muddle the lime wedges and simple syrup. Add the strawberry puree and vodka. Fill the remainder of the shaker with ice. Shake and strain into a baby bottle. Top with champagne (or club soda).

note

This cocktail tastes best on a PJ (private jet). Lala prefers a baby bottle, but you can use a champagne flute.

GLASSWARE

baby bottle

OR

CHAMPAGNE
FLUTE

SPECIAL TOOLS

Cocktail Shaker

Muddler

Sugar Daddy

SPIRITS

PEACH VODKA

CHAMPAGNE

GLASSWARE

SHORT
GLASS

SPECIAL TOOLS

Cocktail Shaker

Muddler

SPIRIT

HENDRICK'S GIN

SORRY NOT SORRY

ARIANA Back in season 4, Kristen apologized to me for some of the things she said about Tom and me. I didn't accept it, and I got so much shit for that. Everyone was telling me I was mean, but I felt it was a bullshit apology. People put so much weight into the words "I'm sorry," when I would rather someone tell me they will never do it again. Show me that you'll never do it again. People say it to absolve themselves for whatever they did, but I think it's often lip service. Tom, on the other hand, loves a sorry. When we're arguing about something, I'll say, "I hear you," so he knows I understand his point of view, but I don't throw out apologies. At the beginning of our relationship, the fights were more common. Now we argue over things like what food we should have delivered for dinner. Tom also wants a foosball table in the living room. I said no. Sorry, not sorry. **SERVES 1**

1 lemon wedge

1 cardamom pod

¾ ounce pear puree
(see opposite)

1½ ounces Hendrick's gin

¾ ounce ruby red grapefruit juice

2 dashes bitters

Club soda

GARNISH: *Lemon twist, rose petals*

In a cocktail shaker, muddle the lemon wedge and cardamom pod with the pear puree. Add the gin, grapefruit juice, and bitters. Fill the remainder of the shaker with ice. Shake and strain over fresh ice in a short glass.

Top with a splash of club soda. Garnish with a lemon twist and rose petals.

note

The pear puree is just like the strawberry puree (page 105). We like to make larger batches of it to have in the freezer for a variety of drinks. You can thaw it out when you need it and it will save you time.

PEAR PUREE

1 pear
2 ounces water
2 ounces Splenda

To make the pear puree, in a blender, combine 1 peeled, cored, and sliced pear with 2 ounces water and 2 ounces Splenda or regular sugar. Blend until smooth and chill until needed.

RADIANT CHILD

ARIANA Absinthe is thought to cause hallucinations. It's also known as "The Green Fairy." I've never actually seen the green fairy when drinking, but maybe you'll have a different experience. Many famous artists drank it back in the day, so we dedicated this cocktail to one of our favorite artists, Jean-Michel Basquiat. **SERVES 1**

1½ ounces absinthe

1½ ounces pineapple juice

¾ ounce lemon juice

1 teaspoon habanero crystals, crushed

Aquafaba (page 58, optional; see note)

GARNISH: 1 teaspoon habanero crystals, crushed (optional)

To a cocktail shaker, add the absinthe, pineapple juice, lemon juice, and habanero crystals. Fill the remainder of the shaker with ice. Shake and strain into martini glass.

note *For a fancy-looking cocktail, top with aquafaba and garnish with habanero crystals. To make a design, use habanero crystals (as seen in photo), pour on top of aquafaba using a stencil to create a design.*

GLASSWARE

MARTINI
GLASS

SPECIAL TOOLS

Cocktail Shaker

Stencil (optional)

SPIRIT

ABSINTHE

GLASSWARE

SHORT
GLASS

SPECIAL TOOL
Cocktail Shaker

SPIRITS
MEZCAL

ROYAL COMBIER

BITTER EX

TOM Everyone knows who my ex-girlfriend is. She's the one who told her boss to "suck a dick," the one who scaled a fence to confront her other ex with his alleged mistress, Hope, and the one who cheated on me while watching *Drive* with my best friend while I was asleep in the next room. To honor my ex, this drink is messy, bitter, spicy, and salty. **SERVES 1**

1 ounce grapefruit juice
Chili salt
1½ ounces mezcal
¾ ounce Royal Combier
½ ounce agave nectar
2 dashes grapefruit bitters

Dampen the rim of a short glass with grapefruit juice. Coat the rim with chili salt.

In a cocktail shaker, combine the remaining grapefruit juice, mezcal, Royal Combier, agave nectar, and grapefruit bitters. Fill the remainder of the shaker with ice. Shake well and strain over fresh ice in the rimmed glass.

note

You can rim the glass with chili salt or ghost pepper salt. Spirit stores typically carry a variety. We recommend something spicy. If you can find the habanero salt and can handle the heat, by all means try that, otherwise chili salt will give it a nice finish.

NICK OF TIME

TOM This one looks like Barbicide, but I promise it tastes better. Speaking of grooming, I got a lot of shit for shaving my forehead on *Vanderpump Rules*. It's actually an old modeling trick. The razor exfoliates the dead skin cells on your face and definitely helps refresh your face when you're hung over. **SERVES 1**

2 ounces vodka

½ ounce blue Curaçao

¾ ounce coconut water

¾ ounce pineapple juice

½ ounce guava juice

½ ounce lemon juice

GARNISH: *Sprig of fresh rosemary, lime slice*

In a cocktail shaker, mix the vodka, Curaçao, coconut water, pineapple juice, guava juice, and lemon juice. Fill the remainder of the cocktail shaker with ice. Shake and strain into tall glass over fresh ice.

Garnish with a sprig of rosemary and a slice of lime.

Guava juice can be tough to find. As always, feel free to sub with your favorite fruit juice or flavors depending on what is in season. The most common substitute for guava is pineapple or strawberries, so we recommend muddling or blending in some strawberries since the recipe already has pineapple juice.

note

DRINK RATING

TRASHY   CLASSY

GLASSWARE

TALL
GLASS

SPECIAL TOOL

Cocktail Shaker

SPIRIT

VODKA

BLUE CURAÇAO

GLASSWARE

CHAMPAGNE

FLUTE

SPECIAL TOOLS

Cocktail Shaker

Muddler

SPIRITS

GIN

LILLET BLANC

CHAMPAGNE

GOLDEN SHOWER

<u>**ARIANA**</u> I love using edible gold dust in cocktails, whether in a garnish or within the drink. It adds a nice sparkle. **SERVES 1**

1 peach, skin removed and pitted

¼ ounce agave nectar

1½ ounces gin

1 ounce Lillet Blanc

½ ounce lemon juice

Champagne

GARNISH: *Edible gold dust*

In a cocktail shaker, muddle the peach with the agave nectar. Add the gin, Lillet Blanc, and lemon juice. Fill the remainder of the cocktail shaker with ice. Shake and strain into Champagne glass. Gently fill to rim with Champagne. Sprinkle with edible gold dust and gently stir into drink.

note

The edible gold dust is found in the cake decorating aisle of your local craft store.

ARIANA'S GO-TO

ARIANA Everyone needs a go-to. I'm talking about a drink that's easy, fresh, and light. I like enough flavor to make it go down easy, but not too much that my taste buds are overwhelmed. This is a twist on a classic vodka soda. Most vodka sodas are served with lime wedges (I think lime in vodka tastes like soap). Lemons are actually the way to go, and I love to add cucumber. If you're out at a crowded bar and the bartenders look stressed and busy, order a vodka soda and ask for lemon and cucumber to garnish. You can use your straw to muddle and mix yourself, and your simple vodka soda will taste a bit less basic. Also, this drink looks like water, so you can drink while you're working . . . if you're into that sort of thing. **SERVES 1**

3 lemon wedges

3 cucumber slices

2½ ounces vodka

Soda water

In a cocktail shaker, muddle the lemon wedges and cucumber slices together. Fill a Collins glass with ice and pour in your favorite vodka. Fill to the top with soda water. Add the muddled lemon wedges and cucumber slices. Mix with the straw.

note

Chances are if you're making this basic go-to, you won't want to dirty a bunch of glasses, but for the best flavor, we recommend muddling separately and then mixing. You can save yourself a step by simply muddling in the serving glass, adding the vodka and ice to that, and mixing with your straw. Don't have a straw? Use your finger. Alcohol disinfects.

DRINK RATING

TRASHY   CLASSY

GLASSWARE

COLLINS
GLASS

SPECIAL TOOLS

Cocktail Shaker

Muddler

Reusable Straw

SPIRIT

VODKA

GLASSWARE

ROCKS
GLASS

SPECIAL TOOLS

Cocktail Shaker

Muddler

Blinky Rings

SPIRITS

GALLIANO

*PEACH
WHISKEY*

BLINKY RING

<u>TOM</u> Whenever we go to a music festival, we buy a bunch of those light-up LED rings, which makes it easier to find friends when they are lost in the crowd. Now that I'm thinking about it, maybe I shouldn't have told you that. Now the festivals are going to be filled with people wearing them. Anyway, this recipe is for all of your music festival needs. The licorice helps when you're peaking and just need something sweet and flavorful. SERVES 1

3 red licorice ropes

⅓ ounce simple syrup (page 17)

¾ ounce Galliano

¾ ounce lime juice

1½ ounces peach whiskey

GARNISH: *Red licorice rope*

In a cocktail shaker, muddle 2 red licorice ropes with the simple syrup. Pour in the Galliano, lime juice, and peach whiskey. Fill the remainder of the shaker with ice. Shake and strain over fresh ice in a rocks glass.

Garnish with remaining red licorice.

note

You can garnish with whatever candy you like. I tend to crave licorice when I'm boozing at a festival.

SOLVANG MELTDOWN

TOM We watch the show along with everyone else. Ariana, of course, told me some of the things that happened on the season 7 girls' trip to Solvang, but it was still exciting to watch it all unfold onscreen. Kristen was messy. She had a bit too much to drink, and she was stumbling around like a baby giraffe with a bone to pick. To honor her Solvang meltdown, I created this special cocktail with a wine base. Be careful . . . this one will hit harder than Kristen's ass hitting the floor as she tries to make a dramatic exit. **SERVES 1**

4 cherries

1½ ounces Merlot

1 ounce bourbon

¼ ounce simple syrup (page 17)

GARNISH: *Grated lemon zest*

In a cocktail shaker, muddle the cherries. Add the Merlot, bourbon, and simple syrup. Add ice to fill the shaker. Shake vigorously to chill. Fill a wine glass with ice cubes and strain the chilled liquid into it.

Use a Microplane zester to grate the lemon zest. Garnish the drink with lemon zest. Drink until you topple over a table.

note

Mixing spirits can be dangerous. This drink has wine and bourbon in it. The cherries and simple syrup will mask a lot of the alcohol flavoring, so just be aware of how much you're drinking. You don't have to topple over that table.

DRINK RATING

TRASHY   CLASSY

GLASSWARE

WINE
GLASS

SPECIAL TOOLS
Cocktail Shaker
Muddler
Microplane Zester

SPIRITS
MERLOT
BOURBON

GLASSWARE

BRANDY SNIFTER

SPECIAL TOOLS

Cocktail Shaker

Melon Baller

SPIRITS

COGNAC

MAD DOG 20/20 ELECTRIC MELON

CHAMPAGNE

THE SIDE HUSTLE

<u>TOM</u> Unless you are a trust fund kid or born into royalty, and the only thing you have to worry about is simply living and breathing, you have to have at least one side hustle in life. Whether it's bartending, acting, or being a foot porn model, make that money! And drink this along the way. **SERVES 1**

2 ounces cognac

1 ounce Mad Dog 20/20 Electric Melon

Champagne

GARNISH: *Melon balls*

In a cocktail shaker, combine the cognac and Mad Dog 20/20. Fill the remainder of the shaker with ice. Shake and strain over fresh ice into a brandy snifter.

Top with Champagne.

Use a melon baller to make 3 melon balls. Garnish drink with melon balls.

note *Watermelon works best for the garnish since it matches the color of the cocktail, but use whatever melon is in season.*

POM PISCO SOUR

ARIANA There's a great guac with pomegranate seeds at a Vanderpump staple, Toca Madera. During season 6, you heard the name "Toca Madera" almost as often as you heard the name "Rob" (Did you know he can hang a TV in less than seven minutes?). I wanted to make a drink that used pomegranate in a different way. If you like sour, this is the drink for you. If you don't want to hear "Toca Madera" ever again, you're gonna have to get them to stop making that bomb guac. **SERVES 1**

2 ounces pisco

¾ ounce lime juice

½ ounce pomegranate juice

½ ounce cardamom agave nectar

¼ ounce egg whites

1 drop bitters (optional)

Add the pisco, lime and pomegranate juices, agave nectar, and egg whites to a cocktail shaker. Fill the remainder of the cocktail shaker with ice. Shake and strain into a coupe glass.

Top with a drop of bitters. Use a toothpick to create a design in the top of the drink.

note *If you don't have egg whites, you can substitute aquafaba page 58).*

DRINK RATING

TRASHY · CLASSY

GLASSWARE

COUPE
GLASS

SPECIAL TOOLS

Cocktail Shaker

Toothpick

SPIRIT

PISCO

PART THREE

Shots

Ice Shot

Ariana If you ever find yourself getting bored with regular shot glasses or you just want to do something cute for a change, try one of these edible shots. Like we said earlier, you can really drink out of anything. Tom made me tequila shots in these ice glasses for my birthday breakfast before we headed out to drink even *more* tequila on our Sonoma NASCAR trip. Typically people bite into a lime wedge after taking tequila shots (which we call "training wheels"), but this time your training wheels are the glasses themselves. They're also great because you can have them in your freezer, ready-to-go, for when friends are over. **MAKES 1 SHOT**

¾ **ounce lime juice**

½ **ounce water**

¼ **ounce simple syrup (page 17)**

1½ **ounces tequila**

Lime wedge

Salt (or use chili salt for extra flavor!)

These ice shot glasses can be customized however you'd like. Fill the molds ¾ of the way with fresh lime juice. Fill the remaining ¼ of the way with water and a few drops of simple syrup. Lightly stir in the mold to mix. The recipe makes one, but most molds will hold 4 to 6.

Place in freezer until frozen, 3 to 4 hours. Carefully remove the shot "glass" from mold. Dampen the rim of the shot glass with the lime wedge. Dip in salt. Fill with chilled tequila.

Note

The shot glass is edible, so take a bite of the lime icicle as a refresher until the next shot!

GLASSWARE

Strawberries

SPECIAL TOOL

Paring knife

Saucepan

SPIRITS

Peach Vodka

Grand Marnier

Strawberry
Gelatin
Shot

Ariana I love a couple things about these strawberry shots. They're delicious and technically healthy because strawberries contain antioxidants, and antioxidants fight free radicals or something. That last part is what I tell myself after I've had a handful. They also look really cute, and they're super easy to make. **MAKES 12 SHOTS**

12 fresh strawberries

½ cup water

1 ounce strawberry gelatin powder

½ cup peach vodka

2 tablespoons Grand Marnier

2 tablespoons lime juice

GARNISH: Dash of chili powder

Using paring knife or strawberry huller, carefully remove the center portions of the strawberries, making sure not to poke through the bottom or sides. Carefully shave off the bottom of the strawberries to level them so they can stand on their own. Set aside on a flat surface until shot mixture is prepared.

Using a saucepan, bring the water to a boil. Reduce the heat and stir in the gelatin powder until dissolved. Stir in the peach vodka, Grand Marnier, and lime juice. Remove from the heat.

Carefully fill the strawberries with the shot mixture. Refrigerate for 3 to 4 hours. Arrange berries on your favorite platter. Garnish with a dash of chili powder and enjoy!

Note

We like spicy mixed with sweet, but if you prefer just the sweet, then forgo the chili powder garnish. Also, these are perfect for a day party because they won't get you too drunk.

Have Your Cake
(But Don't Eat It)

Ariana This is a dessert shot. It tastes rich and creamy. If you're going out after dinner, you don't want a heavy dessert weighing you down. Make this shot instead, so you'll keep the buzz going and you won't want to take a nap. **MAKES 1 SHOT**

¼ ounce Frangelico

¼ ounce citrus-flavored vodka

¼ ounce Baileys Irish Cream

¼ ounce Chambord

Fill a cocktail shaker with ice. Add the Frangelico, vodka, Baileys Irish Cream, and Chambord. Shake. Strain into a chilled shot glass.

Note

This is best using a chilled shot glass, but it's not necessary. Shake extra vigorously with ice in a cocktail shaker if your shot glass isn't chilled.

GLASSWARE

Shot Glass

SPECIAL TOOL

Cocktail Shaker

SPIRITS

Frangelico

Citrus Vodka

Baileys Irish Cream

Chambord

Have Your Cake (But Don't Eat it) *page 169*

Hewes Your Daddy

Tom The holidays are stressful. And busy. Sometimes you need a need a drink to relax, especially all the moms and dads out there. This isn't a holiday-specific shooter, but it is best served in December. The gingerbread liqueur and Baileys will make it feel like Christmas. Serve it at your next party, or take a few while you're wrapping gifts with Santa. **MAKES 1 SHOT**

½ ounce honey whiskey
½ ounce gingerbread liqueur
1 ounce Baileys Irish Cream

Fill a cocktail shaker with ice. Add the whiskey, gingerbread liqueur, and Baileys Irish Cream. Shake. Strain into a shot glass.

Note

You'll find gingerbread liqueur in most grocery and liquor stores around the holidays. This drink is dedicated to our friend and master mixologist Chris Hewes.

DRINK RATING

TRASHY   CLASSY

GLASSWARE

Shot Glass

SPECIAL TOOL

Cocktail Shaker

SPIRITS

Honey Whiskey

Gingerbread Liqueur

Baileys Irish Cream

GLASSWARE

Shot Glass

SPECIAL TOOL

Cocktail Shaker

SPIRITS

Aloe Liqueur

Tequila

Fernet

The Refresher

Tom Aloe liqueur seems to be popping up everywhere these days. It's trendy because it's delicious. It also tastes healthy-ish (as healthy as a shot can taste). This shooter recipe is easy to make, clean, and refreshing. I recommend having the ingredients handy during your next summer picnic. It tastes great by the pool on a hot day. **MAKES 1 SHOT**

½ ounce aloe liqueur

½ ounce tequila

½ ounce fernet

Fill a cocktail shaker with ice. Add the aloe liqueur, tequila, and fernet. Shake. Strain into a shot glass.

Irish Craic

Ariana Craic (pronounced "crack") is not what you're thinking. Or maybe it is. We learned that "craic" means good music, fun, and friends in Ireland. It's meant to define the joy that comes from bringing people together and having a good time. Is it vulgar of us to laugh every time we imagine someone looking for craic? Maybe. Regardless, I love craic. **MAKES 1 SHOT**

1 ounce Irish whiskey

¼ ounce Chambord

¼ ounce ginger liqueur

Fill a cocktail shaker with ice. Add the whiskey, Chambord, and ginger liqueur. Shake. Strain into a shot glass.

Note

The difference between Irish and American whiskey is the primary ingredient. Irish has barley, while American has corn, rye, or wheat.

GLASSWARE

Shot Glass

SPECIAL TOOL

Cocktail Shaker

SPIRITS

Irish Whiskey

Chambord

Ginger Liqueur

GLASSWARE

Shot Glass

SPECIAL TOOL

Cocktail Shaker

SPIRITS

Scotch

Chambord

Red Wine

Champagne

The Promotion

Tom This shot is filled with alcohol you would drink to celebrate getting a promotion. Be proud and buy yourself something nice. **MAKES 1 SHOT**

½ ounce Scotch

½ ounce Chambord

½ ounce red wine

Champagne

Fill a cocktail shaker with ice. Add the Scotch, Chambord, and red wine. Shake. Strain into a shot glass. Top with Champagne.

Note

Don't ever shake Champagne, or it will explode. You always want to be sure to add it into the drink after shaking and straining or mixing gently.

Tomikaze

Tom The buzz button flower is an off-menu item at TomTom. We don't serve it regularly, but whenever I'm there and have friends stop in, I love to make them a Tomikaze, complete with the flower bud. They are always surprised by the flavors.

MAKES 1 SHOT

3 cucumber slices

3 jalapeño slices

½ ounce light agave nectar

¾ ounce St. Germain elderflower liqueur

¾ ounce lemon juice

1½ ounces tequila

Buzz button flower, aka *Acmella oleracea* (optional)

In a cocktail shaker, muddle the cucumber and jalapeño with the agave nectar. Add the St. Germain, lemon juice, and tequila. Fill the remainder of the shaker with ice. Shake and strain into shot glass.

Complete with the buzz button flower, if desired.

Note

The buzz button flower, when chewed, will numb your mouth. It also stimulates the saliva glands. It will naturally cleanse your palate so you'll be able to experience the flavors of the drink more strongly than you would without it. We recommend chewing the buzz button and waiting a few seconds before consuming the liquid. It will feel like a little jolt of electricity in your mouth.

DRINK RATING

TRASHY   CLASSY

GLASSWARE

Shot Glass

SPECIAL TOOL

Cocktail Shaker

Muddler

SPIRITS

St. Germain Elderflower Liqueur

Tequila

GLASSWARE

Shot Glasses

SPECIAL TOOL

Cocktail Shaker

Lighter

SPIRITS

Midori

Absinthe

Green Chartreuse

Reptilian Brain

Tom There was an episode of *Vanderpump Rules* in season 7 where we must've said "reptilian brain" about a thousand times. We were all at Kristen's for a couple's counseling session. That day, Ariana and I had a breakthrough. Viewers might not always understand our relationship, but we understand it. She is the best person I know, and I'm so lucky to have her in my life. She's smart, beautiful, and funny. She centers me, and I like to think I get her out of her shell. If you don't have someone in your life that pushes you out of your comfort zone, have a few of these shots. Three of these babies should do the trick. **MAKES 3 SHOTS**

¾ **ounce Midori**

¾ **ounce absinthe**

¾ **ounce Green Chartreuse**

¾ **ounce lime juice**

GARNISH: **Sugar cube, absinthe (optional)**

Fill a cocktail shaker with ice. Add the Midori, absinthe, Chartreuse, and lime juice. Shake. Strain into three shot glasses.

For garnish, carefully dip the sugar cube in absinthe. Light the cube on fire.

Note

Be VERY careful when lighting the garnish on fire. Don't do it unless you're sure of yourself!

Disco Tits

Ariana It's no secret I've had body issues. I think a lot of women can relate. When I was in seventh grade, a boy broke up with me because he said I had mosquito bites for boobs. Years later I dated a guy who would tell me not to wear shorts. When I got on television, I started hearing from strangers who would comment on my Instagram when my legs looked bigger than normal, or they would try to tear me down by commenting on my body. All that shit adds up. The good thing about dating Tom is that he loves me for who I am, not what I look like. He's happy if I'm happy. Growing up, and going to therapy, has helped me embrace what I look like and ignore the comments. Some of the self-doubt is still there, but there are times I feel free of it. Recently, I was at a music festival and I took off my shirt and put on some body paint, glitter and jewels. There was a moment where I was listening to Tove Lo's "Disco Tits" with no top, just gold body paint, where I felt totally free. Those moments can be few and far between, but I've learned to take note of them. **MAKES 1 SHOT**

¾ ounce vodka

¾ ounce St. Germain elderflower liqueur

½ ounce lemon juice

GARNISH: **Edible gold dust**

Fill a cocktail shaker with ice. Add the vodka, St. Germain, and lemon juice. Shake. Strain into a shot glass. Garnish with edible gold dust.

Note

You can purchase edible gold dust at a craft store. Look for it in the aisle with the baking supplies. They have a variety of colors.

GLASSWARE

Shot Glasses

SPECIAL TOOLS

Mixing Bowl

Refrigerator

SPIRIT

Jägermeister

Jäger Bomb
Gelatin

Ariana Jäger bombs are a party staple, but traditional Jäger bombs can get messy. You end up with broken glasses and sticky surfaces. These gelatin shots take the mess out of the equation and you can pre-mix.

    Tom If your guests are bored, you need to give them one of these. Shots are a fun group activity, and these are loaded with energy drink, so they will help everyone get hype. **MAKES 12 SHOTS**

JÄGER GELATIN

¼ **cup boiling water**

¼ **cup Jägermeister**

½ **packet unflavored gelatin powder**

ENERGY DRINK GELATIN

¼ **cup boiling water**

¼ **cup energy drink**

½ **packet unflavored gelatin powder**

For the Jäger Gelatin: In a mixing bowl, combine the boiling water, Jägermeister, and gelatin powder. Mix until dissolved. Let cool slightly. Fill 12 shot glasses halfway with the Jäger gelatin mix. Chill the shots in the refrigerator for 20 minutes.

    For the Energy Drink Gelatin: In a mixing bowl, combine the boiling water, energy drink, and gelatin powder. Mix until dissolved. Let cool slightly.

    Remove the chilled shot glasses from refrigerator. Fill the shot classes with energy gelatin mix not quite all the way to the top. Place the shots back in the refrigerator and let sit for 3 to 4 hours. The shots should have 2 clear layers in same shot glass.

Note

You don't want to fill these shot glasses all the way to the top. With gelatin shots, you need some space to put your finger in so you can scoop out the shot. These will give you energy, so don't take right before bed.

Melted Snowman

Tom This is an old bartending trick. When your friends want to take shots, but you know you've already had too much to drink, order or make a melted snowman shot. It's literally just a shot of water. Calling it a melted snowman will confuse your friends, and they will think you're drinking something fancier than you are. They'll be having lemon drops while you suck down some H_2O. You'll hydrate and, hopefully, have a slightly more manageable hangover the next day. **SERVES 1**

1½ ounces water

Fill a shot glass with water. Drink. Make another. Drink.

 Know when to cut yourself off. Sloppy drunks are fun to watch on TV, but it's never fun to be the sloppy drunk in real life. Drink responsibly and hydrate often.

GLASSWARE

Shot Glass

SPECIAL TOOL

You're a special tool. That's why we're cutting you off.

SPIRIT
You've had enough.

PART FOUR

RECOVERY

TRIP THE LIGHT

ARIANA This is a virgin drink to help aid in recovery. I recommend using it to wash down a Midol Complete. You can also make a batch in the blender the night before, so you have it ready in the a.m. when you need it most. **Serves 1**

GLASSWARE

SHORT GLASS

1¼ ounces watermelon (roughly 4 ice cream scoops of watermelon)

1¼ ounces cantaloupe (roughly 4 ice cream scoops of cantaloupe)

4 slices cucumber

4 ounces coconut water

½ ounce fresh lemon juice

Splash of soda water

Dash of cayenne

2 Midol Complete (optional)

SPECIAL TOOLS

Ice Cream Scoop

Blender

Use the ice cream scoop to measure the watermelon and cantaloupe. Put in a blender. Add the cucumber, coconut water, lemon juice, splash of soda, and dash of cayenne. Blend. Pour into a short glass.

Chase Midol with the drink (or toss it in the blender with everything else).

SPIRIT

NONE

NOTE

Everyone always asks us the best hangover remedy. Men might be too shy to buy it, but Midol Complete is great for women and men. It has an antihistamine, pain reliever, and caffeine. Take the pill, go back to sleep, and you'll hop out of bed 30 minutes later, ready to face the day.

TRIP THE LIGHT PAGE 192

DRINK RATING

TRASHY   CLASSY

GLASSWARE

COUPE GLASS

SPECIAL TOOL

Cocktail Shaker

SPIRITS

CHAMBORD

TENNESSEE WHISKEY

LEGGO MY EGO

TOM This is a hair-of-the-dog drink. As I got older, I noticed my hangovers were getting worse. I didn't want to admit it because of my ego. We can't stay young forever. Waking up after a night of drinking can be painful, but if you make this breakfast cocktail, at least you can drink your waffles and eat your omelet, too. **Serves 1**

⅓ ounce honey
¾ ounce Chambord
2 ounces Tennessee whiskey

2 dashes vanilla bitters
1 large egg
GARNISH: Waffle, maple syrup

In a cocktail shaker, combine the honey, Chambord, whiskey, bitters, and whole egg. Shake without ice (this is a dry shake). Fill the remainder of the cocktail shaker with ice. Strain into a coupe glass. Garnish with a slice of waffle drizzled with maple syrup.

NOTE

This one you want to shake without ice because we don't want the ice to change the consistency of the egg. For the garnish, we used a tiny piece of a waffle and drizzled it with maple syrup. Eat the rest of the waffle before you start boozing again if you if you want to last the whole day. If you want to get drunk again, bypass the waffle and make it a double.

RACE DAY CLASSIC
BLOODY MARY

ARIANA We mentioned earlier we love the Kentucky Derby. I grew up watching it on TV every year. Mint julep is the traditional track drink, but my mom would make bloody marys. If there's one thing I learned from Tanya Madix, it's that you *must* have Old Bay Seasoning in your bloody mary. This is also a perfect hair-of-the-dog drink if you wake up with a hangover. The saltiness of the olives and tomato juice will aid in recovery, and the vodka will get you drunk again. **Serves 1**

Lime wedge

Old Bay Seasoning

2 ounces vodka

2 ounces Clamato juice

¼ ounce lime juice

½ ounce lemon juice

4 drops hot sauce

Dash of celery salt

Cracked black peppercorns

GARNISH: *Celery, green olive, bacon, mozzarella, leftover lime wedge*

Dampen the rim of a highball glass with a lime wedge. Dip the rim into the Old Bay Seasoning. Fill the rimmed highball glass with ice. Add the vodka, Clamato juice, lime juice, lemon juice, hot sauce, and celery salt. Stir. Top with the cracked peppercorns.

To garnish, load a skewer with the celery, green olive, bacon, mozzarella, and leftover lime wedge from rimming the glass.

NOTE

Bloody mary garnishes are a breakfast free-for-all. You can add hard-boiled eggs, pickles, peppers, honestly whatever the f*ck you want to eat that day you can throw on a spear and chase it with your bloody mary. Invite your friends over and have a bloody mary bar set up with all your favorites.

DRINK RATING

TRASHY   CLASSY

GLASSWARE

HIGHBALL GLASS

SPECIAL TOOL

Skewer

SPIRIT

VODKA

RECOVERY — PAGE NO.

GLASSWARE

*TALL
GLASS*

SPECIAL TOOL

Blender

SPIRIT

VODKA
(optional)

SMOOTHIE CRIMINAL

ARIANA This is a true recovery cocktail. If you wake up with that hangover stomach feeling and a headache, this will help. I like the mix of strawberries, peach, bananas, and goji berries, but anything you have will do if you're desperate and only have a few of the fruits. Tom and I keep a bag of flax seed for this drink and we add just a small handful in. You can also add those electrolyte packets into the mix. **Serves 1**

5 strawberries

1 peach, peeled, cored, and cut into chunks

1 banana, cut into chunks

10 goji berries

1 teaspoon flax seed

1 cup coconut water

1 ounce vodka (optional)

GARNISH: 2 Midol Complete (optional)

Combine all ingredients in a blender and blend together until smooth. Stir in an ounce of vodka, depending on the level of hangover.

Consume ASAP directly from blender (or pour into a glass if you prefer). Use as a chaser for Midol.

NOTE

If you want a classic recovery drink, make this sans vodka. If you want a hair-of-the-dog/morning after drink, then add the vodka. Both make for a great lunch!

ACKNOWLEDGMENTS

We could talk about the wonderful people in our lives for days. This is really just a snippet of the gratitude we have for all of those who have helped shape this book, our years behind the bar, and our lives. We are so incredibly lucky to know all of you and we hope to make you proud. Thank you for drinking our drinks over all these years!

Our parents: Terri, Tanya, Anthony, Jim, and Mike. You guys believe in us when we find it hard to believe in ourselves. You push us to be the best versions of ourselves by setting such amazing examples for us. You constant sources of inspiration. We were born lucky simply because we had you all to raise us. We love you so much and wish that we could all be here together. You can't pick your family, and we still ended up with two of the best families anyone could ever ask for.

Danny Pellegrino, let it be known: You are too funny, too kind, too good-looking, and too talented to be one person. It's not fair to the rest of us, but we don't care because we are all lucky to know you. We can't imagine what this book or this life would be like without you in it—and thankfully, we don't have to.

Photoshoot Crew, aka The Dream Team, aka the best group of people ever assembled . . .

Kelly Puleio, the most unbelievably talented photographer and awesome human.

Tamara Costa, thank you for making all of our visions happen and keeping us all from falling apart.

Maxwell Smith, production designer and coolest person in the room.

Nicola Parisi, photo assistant and beautiful human.

Avery Ferguson, prop assistant and ball of positive light.

Kelly Fallon, prop assistant with the best hair ever.

Mo Hodges, cocktail stylist and who we all want to be when we grow up.

Jared Lipscomb, makeup artist and number-one giggle fit inducer.

Bradley Leake, hair magician who gives us so much confidence when we need it most.

Kasra Ajir, thank you for believing in me since day one, when I couldn't afford to even eat, much less pay you a dime. Here's to many more years together.

David Doerrer, we wouldn't be here without you! Thank you for taking us on and making it happen.

Justin Schwartz and **HMH,** thank you so much for trusting us and encouraging us along the way. You've made a couple of lifelong dreams come true.

Ryan Pastorek, thank you for always being in our corner.

Jeremy Madix and **Fortune Films, BTS Film,** and the best little brother in the entire world.

John Frietas and **Fresh Origins Microgreens,** you always inspire and motivate us with your knowledge and passion.

Kyle Chan, jewelry designer, your talent and generosity knows no bounds.

Tyler Everhart, we couldn't have done these looks without you!

Tom Schwartz, one half of the greatest bromance of our time and a truly great friend to all.

Josh Ahrens, thank you for going all over town to keep us from falling apart mid-shoot!

Meredith Brace Sloss, best friendship and best iced coffee morale boosts when we needed it most.

Logan Cochran, because of you, I'm stronger. I catch my breath knowing my life would suck without you. Thank you for being there!

Ali Rafiq and **Zach Siegfried,** who Tom kept up until 5 a.m. making sure he made his deadline.

Echo Inc., for the sexy-ass chainsaws.

Chris Hewes, thank you for consulting.

Doug McFarland, thank you for being a friend.

Adam Ambrose, Lauren Johnson, Ryan Revel, Joe Weiner, thank you for being such a strong team.

Andy Cohen, Lisa Vanderpump, Ken Todd, and the **entire cast of Vanderpump Rules,** for inspiring us, fighting with us, and partying with us.

Fans of Vanderpump Rules, for believing in us and trolling us when we get annoying. We love all of you, even if you make fun of us on social media.

Evolution Media and **Bravo,** for allowing us to tell our stories and connect with people everywhere.

Tom would like to thank Ariana for being the most amazing person and the best damn Dumplin' in the whole wide world. You're my beautiful information booth and you always make me smile. I love you so much.

Ariana would like to thank Tom for being such an incredible partner and friend, in life and in love. Thank you for challenging me to grow and loving me for all that I am. I am so proud of you and can't wait for what's next. You also look pretty great in drag.

Danny would like to thank Ariana and Tom for being the best and taking me on this ride, plus everyone that helped bring this project to life. Thanks to Linda, Gary, Matt, Jr., Bryan, Taryn, Sam, Anth, Bella, Soph, and Brady Pellegrino for being the greatest family in the world.

SPIRITS

INDEX

ARIANA MADIX is one of the stars of *Vanderpump Rules* on Bravo. Before being seen bartending at SUR and Villa Blanca on the show, she was mixing drinks at some of the most popular establishments in New York and Los Angeles. Madix is from Melbourne, Florida, and currently lives in Los Angeles with Tom. After a few cocktails, she can be found waxing poetic about "Yellow Robe Smith" . . . whatever that is.

TOM SANDOVAL is one of the original cast members of Bravo's *Vanderpump Rules*. He is the co-owner of TomTom, which was named Best Bar in Southern California by *Los Angeles Travel Magazine* in 2019. Sandoval was born in St. Louis before beginning a successful modeling career that took him to New York, Los Angeles, Miami, and Chicago. He spends his free time flawlessly playing his trumpet, and he looks stunning in drag.

DANNY PELLEGRINO is an author, comedian, and screenwriter living in Los Angeles. He created and hosts the hit podcast *Everything Iconic with Danny Pellegrino*. The Cleveland native has performed sold-out shows across the country, and lends his pop culture expertise to various projects. On most nights he can be found watching Bravo shows from his bed with a glass of bed-wine.